ANGELS
IN
CHARGE

Jacqueline M. Emmens

Published by Jacqueline M. Emmens
ISBN: 0 9530849 0 6

Books may be ordered from:

Mrs J. M. Emmens
P.O. Box 4,
Exmouth,
Devon, EX8 4SH,
England, U.K.
Tel: 01395 279695

or

Mr. & Mrs. B. Maxey,
2809 Frazier Road,
Hartford,
AR 72938.
U.S.A.
Tel: 501 928 7091

Printed in England by Clays Ltd, St Ives plc

I dedicate this book to Gordon, my dear husband. Also to the memory of our three children, now with Jesus, and to Linda our remaining daughter. They had to endure long periods of separation from us, because of the work.

I wish also to express our gratitude to all people who have helped and supported us through the years.

Our thanks go to Sonia Gough, in Wales, Judy Bird and Denise Fernald in Utopia, U.S.A., who have helped me to get the book into shape and on to computer and finally to Dean Holling, of South Chard Fellowship, England, U.K., for his cover design.

FOREWORD

"For He shall give His angels charge over thee,
to keep thee in all thyways" (Ps 91:11)

"Angels in Charge" was the title impressed on me as I considered what I should call the book. It comes from the 11th verse of the 91st Psalm, which we used to call our air-raid shelter during World War II.

The study of the ministry of angels is fascinating. One Scripture declares that the angels are ministering spirits (servants), sent out to serve those who will inherit salvation. It is also affirmed that each of us has a ministering angel constantly in attendance (Matt.18:10)

Many are the stories of missionaries and others who have known the intervention of angels in their lives - often in times of crisis. It seems that they can take on the form of humans, on occasion.

Gordon and I are convinced that angels have played a great part in our lives, and we thank God for their ministry. I believe that He wants people to know of the existence of these wonderful beings and that is why I was directed to Ps.91 at the commencement of this book.

CONTENTS

ONE

"STORMCHILD"

It was Easter 1942, and I was in a village called Fyfield in Essex. Just ten days previously I had been in London which was being bombed continually by the Germans. As I lay on the couch by the fire, I thought back on my life and the events that had led to my being here.

I dimly remembered my mother and incidents of my early life with her. My father had not been living with us for some time and only a couple of scenes in which he had been present stood out in my memory. One of those, when I was three, and had scribbled with a crayon all round our newly papered living-room. Father's reactions were painful for me! The other took place about six months later, when he came to pick me up for our weekly outing. Mother had cried.

Sickness seemed to play a big part in our lives. We were always visiting the doctor or hospital. When I was barely five, I was put into a hospital under observation because of a large goitre. It was mother's turn next. She had developed tuberculosis while father was still with us.

He had sent us to the south of France to help her fight the disease but while we were away he met my step-mother to be. He had moved out of the apartment to live with her, and the shock of his departure set mother right back. She lost the will to live. While she was in the hospital I was sent to live with an aunt. I didn't see much more of her after that.

Poor mother. She was French and had been sent to friends in England by my grandparents at the onset of the first world war, when the Germans invaded Belgium. She and her twin sister had been in a convent there. The sister returned to France at the end of the war but mother had met and married my father. Both had come from strict religious families and had turned against the restrictions of their early lives; mother against the Roman Catholic church and father against the Salvation Army and Evangelical Bible Class. Together they embarked on a life in London which had no place for religion.

Father had been badly wounded in the war and his recovery, was agreed by all to be a miracle, which inclined him at first to return to the faith of his parents. Mother, however, had laughed at him and teased him away, something for which she was to be deeply sorry later on.

Mother, being very clever, had succeeded in finishing her education in England and, qualifying in the scientific field, became an analytical chemist. She worked in a laboratory and then in translating until her marriage. Not being very domesticated, she was unable to play the role expected of her by my father who had been spoilt as a result of being the youngest son and a wounded war hero. The domestic happiness did not last long and mother subsequently died at the age of twenty-eight. Her family had cut her off when she had failed to have me baptized in the Roman Catholic church; Deserted by family and husband she succumbed to the illness that had attacked her lungs.

I was five and a half when some relative came one day to tell me that mother had been carried to heaven by the angels. She had passed away in the home of my English grandparents who had faithfully cared for her in her last days, helping her to a saving faith in Jesus before she drew her last painful breath. For two years I doggedly maintained to my friends that mother hadn't been buried in a church yard like other people, but had been taken straight to heaven by two angels. I remember often looking through the window at the stars at night and wishing that God would send her back.

Visits from my father were rare. He had married again, soon after my mother's death. His new wife was pretty and smelled so nice when she kissed me but they never took me home with them after these visits. However, I was told they lived in my old house but that it was better for me to stay with my aunt near the country, away from the unhealthy city. Remembering the high buildings and noisy traffic, I accepted what they said philosophically.

My weekends had to be spent with two other "aunties" whom I was told were my guardians. The young woman who worked for them, a buxom country girl called Ruth, used to fetch me on Saturday evening and take me to their home above the Art Supply shop, where she put me to bed. She would wake me very early on Sunday morning and sit by me trying to coax me to eat some breakfast while I was still half asleep. The younger aunt would then drive us to their little house in the country. It was only one and a half hours away but it seemed such a long journey. Tucked up in a rug, sitting between two Pekinese dogs and Ruth, I was invariably car-sick.

When we arrived we always had a cup of tea before freshening up to go the the local Anglican church. The ancient organ was pumped by a boy, working at the lever at the side of it. Although I was still feeling rather miserable, watching him made me forget my boredom. If he didn't pump hard enough the organ would run down and my aunts would sing all the louder to try and keep the congregation from going flat! How relieved I was when the service ended! Usually by the time we had walked home to lunch, I would feel much better and would enjoy a meal. We would go for a long walk in the afternoon, during part of which I would be pushed in an ancient push-chair, and then we would visit some of the aunts' relatives who owned the village shop. The next morning I would be driven home early, in time for school.

I was a 'delicate' child, and was sent to a small private school for two years. The three maiden ladies who ran it were sisters and they had two beautiful St. Bernard dogs. I used to think that the youngest sister looked just like the dogs - she was big, slow and had heavy jowls. However, they were all very kind to me and I enjoyed school. It was there that I became enlightened as to my mother's death and burial.

My musing was interrupted by the entrance of Mabel, carrying our evening drinks. Mabel was a quiet, middle-aged spinster, old-fashioned in appearance but oh, so kind and gentle - so different from my younger guardian, who was tall and rather domineering with a loud penetrating voice. Her mother was a gentle lady though. Mabel had come to live in the house, where she did domestic chores and cooking at weekends and holidays, in exchange for her room and keep. She was now taking care of me and sent me off to bed as soon as we had finished our drinks.

When I was settled in bed, my thoughts returned to my early years again. As I grew older I did not accompany my guardians so often, and on Sunday I was sent to a Methodist Sunday School, later joining the choir. One Sunday afternoon an evangelist spoke to us. When he made an appeal for those who wanted to ask Jesus into their hearts, I put my hand up. I was about eleven at the time. However, no one spoke to me about my commitment afterwards.

Life went on as usual and I forgot about this experience. Several of my relatives were professing Christians but they didn't impress me. I liked the non-christians more and despised the others for being narrow and old-fashioned. From what I could see, Christianity seemed to be a list of "don'ts"! However, my grandmother was an exception. She was a true saint, but although I loved and admired her I didn't want to be altogether like her! She was a peacemaker and never raised her voice, never stood up for herself. She always said "Yes, dear," and "No, dear," to my grandfather. I decided I did not want to be such a submissive wife.

My grandparents had been officers in the Salvation Army in the days of General Booth. In fact, grandfather had been his Adjutant for a time. Grandmother had joined as a girl. She was the daughter of a well-to-do farmer from a respectable Methodist family and had been the belle of the Suffolk County. It was difficult to imagine my ladylike grandmother preaching in the open-air meetings outside rowdy taverns in slum districts! She told me she once had a batter pudding mixture poured over her as she was doing visitation work!

I could see grandfather as an Army Officer. Erect, soldierly and rather stern in appearance, with thick iron-grey wavy hair and clipped moustache, he was a good-looking man. Later, they had resigned from their position in the Army and grandfather went into business with his cousin. He didn't approve of the methods developed by the Army of soliciting finances. However, they still attended the local "Citadel', as the meeting place of the Army was called, on Sunday morning. In the evening we went to the more intellectually-inclined Congregational church.

I had to go to church three times on a Sunday, while living with my grandparents. It was the Army in the morning, the Methodist Sunday School in the afternoon and the Congregational church at night. How I envied my school friends, whose parents let them lie in bed on Sunday mornings and took them pleasure-riding in the car in the afternoon! I attended a girls' school for the daughters of professional people, and my companions were rather inclined to look down upon the Army.

One Sunday morning I had been rather puzzled by the preacher who had talked a lot about "the blood", and I asked my grandfather to explain it. Rather brashly I had said that I couldn't understand the God of the Old Testament - He seemed so gory! Grandfather said, "Yours is not to reason why, yours is but to do or die!" What an opportunity he missed! If only he had explained that the sacrifices of animals in the Old Testament for the sins of the people were types that fore-shadowed the death of Jesus, who was the Supreme Sacrifice for our sin. Being about twelve years old at the time, I could have understood the depth of meaning in the Scriptures showing forth the value of the blood of Jesus that "cleanses from all sin" (I John 1:7).

Grandfather, having a Victorian attitude towards children, didn't realize that a young, enquiring mind had to 'know the reason why'! How I thank God that He has said, "Come let us <u>reason</u> together, though your sins be scarlet they shall be white as snow!"

However, although appearing to be rather distant and awe

inspiring he was kindly and I remember hearing him praying every morning as I tiptoed past his bedroom on my way to the bathroom. He was a man of integrity and was highly respected by his business associates.

My bachelor uncle and spinster aunt also lived with their parents. Uncle was a quiet, studious man and an artist. He went to an Evangelical Mission and used to talk with grandfather about the coming judgements of God as taught in the Bible. He was always very pessimistic, and rather flippantly I used to call him the prophet of doom! My aunt, who lost her fiancé in the First World War was "highly strung" and a terrible nagger. Nothing could be left out of place in the house so I was always in trouble. She and uncle used to talk in dark tones about my future, as during my teens boyfriends came to the house to see me. I was a 'flirt' they said.

During this period I was allowed to spend some vacations with my father and his wife. What a contrast to my grandparents' home! Card parties in the house and an occasional dinner out, when I was allowed a glass of wine. Of course I was told not to tell about this to the folk at home or I wouldn't be allowed to visit again! According to the Salvation Army, people who did such things would go to hell. Even my aunt and uncle frowned on father's way of life.

"Just wait until I'm old enough to leave home. No more church for me," I thought. "Dad's friends are much more fun and so are my worldly school friends! My relatives and their circle are right out of date". By this time all I'd learned about evolution and geology research had helped to reinforce my opinions. Even the Methodist minister who was accepted as a real scholar didn't accept the Bible teaching on creation. I began to feel ashamed of my enforced visits to the Salvation Army as my friends mocked it.

One morning however, when I was about fourteen, a new Salvation Army Major came to take charge of the Citadel. He spoke with great clarity and his words seemed to be directed straight at me. "Robbing God" had been the central theme of his message one particular Sunday morning. Afterwards he made an appeal for people to surrender their lives to Him. I felt really uncomfortable! The afternoon when I had said "yes" to a similar appeal, had been forgotten but then it came back to me. Into my mind flooded all the things I wanted to do when I left school - the operas, theatres and classical music I wanted to enjoy. How I looked forward to the freedom to find my own life-style, loosened from the narrow-minded customs that so restricted me in my suburban environment!

So I deliberately hardened my heart to the Major's plea and to the convicting voice of the Holy Spirit. "Not now," I thought. "When I am older, maybe. I just can't become a member of the Salvation Army and conform to their killjoy religion. Life had something greater for me than that. I don't really belong to this uncultured, crude set-up." What a snob I had become!

I was relieved when we were able to get up and go, but I couldn't look the officer in the eyes when he shook hands with us at the door. My grandparents were disappointed, I knew, and I could feel the disapproval of my grandfather.

According to my relatives, I was self-willed and rebellious. Grandfather called me "stormchild'. Not knowing I was within earshot, my uncle once said to my aunt, "With Violet having been so French, vivacious and attractive, and Harry such a man-about-town, (referring to my parents) what can you expect?"

Naturally, I was always anxious to learn about my mother. They told me she was not religious, although she had come from a strong Catholic background. It appeared that, being an avid reader and of an enquiring mind, mother had read certain books forbidden by the Catholic church. Her conscience pricking her, she had confessed this to the priest. He, being a friend of the family, broke the regulations and informed her parents, which resulted in trouble for mother! When she came to England, she was not interested in maintaining attendance at the Roman Catholic church.

I drifted into sleep, awakening in the morning to the sound of . birds and Mabel, bustling around in the kitchen. Thanking God for bringing me here, my thoughts went back to the year before the war.

The time had come for me to leave my grandparents and live with their youngest daughter, who had become Assistant Director of an Orthopaedic clinic in Birmingham. They thought she was better equipped to cope with a teenager! This aunt had cared for me when I was a baby and mother had become ill. Auntie Edith had given up her job so that she could look after me. Being still only seventeen herself, she had dedicated herself so completely to my care for six months, that she developed gastric trouble, from which she suffered for years. Throughout my childhood she had sacrificed so that I could have the good schooling that my pleasure-loving stepmother prevented my father from giving me. Naturally I was very fond of my young aunt. I certainly enjoyed a greater freedom while with her, and happily pursued my studies and various interests.

World War II then erupted and disturbed our pleasant lives. I did a First Aid course at the local swimming baths, which had been turned into a Casualty Center and took my turn at helping man the Center. However, my aunt became worried because we were living too near a large factory that had been turned over to make war equipment. The Germans had started their bombing raids on the Midlands, where there were so many of these factories. At this point of time, I also had a succession of boyfriends, which caused her some anxiety, especially as she was then taken up with a doctor friend of her own! She therefore decided that it was time my father assumed responsibility for me and sent me to live with him and his wife in central London.

On my arrival in London, I went to work at the headquarters of the British Red Cross. I joined the central Y.W.C.A. Club and the choir of a nearby Church of England, which had lost half its choir owing to the recent evacuation of all the children under 16. My father had persuaded me to take this latter step, hoping that the church would exercise a good influence on me! My interest was solely in the music and I had been told that the choirmaster was a very dedicated and able man, with a high standard for his choir. After a short period it was suggested that I should train under a well known singer, as he thought I had a promising voice. I became a regular visitor to the Sadlers Wells Opera House, concerts and so forth. My life was quite full and enjoyable, in spite of the war.

Before leaving Birmingham I had formed a special attachment to a particular boyfriend who was an engineering apprentice. He missed me a lot and decided to join the R.A.F. to train as a pilot. As he was then stationed not far from London, he was able to visit me quite regularly.

When I was about eight years old, I had been operated on for a large goitre on my thyroid. Unfortunately, six months later I had caught the whooping-cough and the strain of coughing had caused the goitre to grow again. Now after nearly nine years of being embarrassed by the unsightly growth, the specialist we consulted advised me to have it removed. The operation went well and I was able to resume normal life. Then the situation changed dramatically. The Germans started to bomb London!

TWO

"ANGELS GUIDE MY FOOTSTEPS"

The sirens wailed their warning several times a day and we were running in and out of the shelters. Sometimes we lay flat on the ground, unable to reach the shelter in time, and watched the fight above us between the English and German 'planes. Starting about eight in the evening, waves of bombers came over throughout the night, dropping their lethal loads. Casualties were very high.

Because we were getting so little sleep at night, father obtained a place for us to sleep in the vaults of a nearby bank and our beds were taken there. However, the other occupants started holding noisy parties and it was decided that we should return home to sleep in our first floor apartment, and 'take a chance'. Father's philosophy was that if a bomb had your name on it, you would 'get it' wherever you were!

Our apartment was one of a large block, built round a central courtyard, and right behind St. Pancras Town Hall, which was opposite the railway station. We were in the vicinity of two main-line stations and therefore a prime target for the bombs. Naval anti-aircraft guns placed in the street added to the noise. The destruction was terrible, especially during the night when the Germans used incendiary bombs.

Many buildings round the British Red Cross headquarters were destroyed and the windows were blown in by the blast of the bombs. It was decided to evacuate the offices and staff to the country. I wouldn't go because father wouldn't leave London, so I transferred to the office of a large pharmaceutical company, which was just a few minutes walk from home. Transport was often difficult to obtain. I had one very sobering experience before I left the Red Cross.

Every morning I would catch a bus at the same time. One morning I reached the bus-stop only to see my bus leaving, which meant that I had to go by the Underground. As I came up out of the station, I heard the scream of a bomb and fell flat on my face on the pavement. We had had no warning siren but these things happened during the early days of the bombing - odd 'planes got through without detection. Later that morning I learned that this bomb had landed on the bus I had missed!

One night especially came to mind. After many nerve-wracking days and nights, my father decided that we had to have a break and said that we would go out to dinner in the West-end the next evening. We duly arrived at one of his favourite eating-places early in the evening, being mindful of the expected waves of bombers later on, and had a delicious dinner. After weeks of subsisting on meager rations, we thoroughly enjoyed it. Just as we finished, the air-raid siren went. An anxious waiter urged father to settle the bill and hurry out to the shelter. Father said we would go home before the raids got under way and called a taxi. When told of our destination the cabby at first refused to go but Dad managed to bribe him.

We heard the bombers above us and the taxi started bouncing as the bombs landed. When we were almost home, there was a terrible noise and the taxi rose in the air, shaking the breath out of us as it landed. "Gawd knows what that was," said the cabby. " I ain't going no further!" We had stopped near a public house and he shouted to us to go down into their cellars. Then he turned the taxi and sped off. "Can any of you do first-aid?" called a voice from the depths of the pub. "I can," I replied, as I ran over and down into the cellar, followed rather unwillingly by my father and step-mother. A group of people sat huddled there, while some casualties, brought in from the street, lay on the floor or sat up holding injured limbs. I was given the rather sparse first-aid kit and hot water and set to work. As the bombs landed round us, bottles of beer shot out of their racks and women screamed, while the men cursed. I had barely finished binding up the last wound when the ambulance men arrived. How tired they looked and yet the night had barely begun! There were still several hours ahead of us during which the bombs would subject us to their merciless attacks.

The ambulance men complimented me on my work as I reported to them what I had done, according to my assessment of each case. The most seriously wounded ones were taken away first while we made the others as comfortable as possible until the ambulance should be able to return for them. We were told that a land-mine had fallen nearly half a mile away from us and that about everything within a radius of that distance had been flattened.

My father was keen to get out of the atmosphere of the cellar. He refused to let me help with any other casualties, saying that I had done enough for one night, considering I was only seventeen and a half and hadn't long been out of hospital myself. He wanted to leave the claustrophobic atmosphere of the cellar and go home, whatever was happening outside! As we made our way out, we found three dustbin lids to hold over our heads to give us a little protection from the shrapnel and, taking advantage of a momentary lull in the screaming bombs, we ran to our apartment block.

When we got to our home, we found that the front door had been jammed by bomb-blast but Dad managed to get it open, eventually. We were so tired that we just fell on our beds and went straight to sleep!

By this time, I had become a volunteer hostess at the Y.W.C.A., and was on the Program committee. Girls on leave from the Forces needed a place to come for relaxation. Our underground swimming-pool had been turned into an air-raid shelter. We all grew accustomed to finding our way round in the black-out at night.

I had one anxiety - Roy, my boyfriend, had gained his wings, becoming a fighter pilot. When on leave, he would tell me of his experience at the airfield. Night after night, he and his colleagues would go up to meet the invaders as well as during the day. Morning after morning, they would see the vacant places at breakfast, previously occupied by fellow pilots. Then he was sent to Canada to be trained as a bomber pilot and I threw myself more and more into various activities so as not to have time to worry.

By then the balloon barrage had been set up round London so less time was spent in the air raid shelters. However, some 'planes still got in and night after night the underground railway stations were filled with people waiting for the trains to stop, in order that they could spread covers over the platforms on which to sleep. Some bombs even penetrated there, causing many deaths.

Then the Y.M.C.A. was bombed to the ground. From then on, young men on leave from the Forces were sent over to us, to feed and entertain. I found myself teaching French-Canadians to dance - in army boots! Some just wanted to sit and chat. I heard stories of war from all fronts, from Australians, New Zealanders, Canadians, Poles, and Frenchmen. The latter had escaped from the Germans and joined our Forces. Some of the Poles had come from Warsaw and had witnessed the atrocities committed there, sometimes seeing their own relatives being shot. These were not interested in any of our activities but would sit in groups, drinking, talking about what they would do to the Germans and vowing a deadly vengeance. Many young men came from training camps on the outskirts of London, and would be regular visitors for several months until their training was at an end, when they would be posted off to join the fighting units. I often wondered, how many of them would return?

THREE

*"I WALK THROUGH THE VALLEY OF THE
SHADOW OF DEATH" (PS.32:4)*

Another tumour was growing in my thyroid and I had to have a third operation, just fourteen months after my last one. Before I left the hospital, a member of the medical staff came to see me. He told me that my vocal chords had been damaged during the course of the operation and that, as a result I would never be able to sing again. He also told me it would be necessary for me to undergo deep x-ray treatment at the Cancer Hospital, because of the malignancy of the last tumour.

The bottom had fallen completely out of my world! I had continued my singing practice, however irregularly, throughout the months of air-raids, my teacher coming to London to give lessons when it was possible. I was considering making a career of singing after the war as it had become the greatest joy of my life. Now this dream was destroyed.

By the time the treatment had ended, I was but a shadow of my former self. The sights I had seen at the Cancer Hospital had left me feeling very depressed. My stepmother didn't like even the mention of hospitals, so I had had to go daily for the treatment on my own, not even being able to speak of the experience.

Life at home was not very happy so I tried to resume my normal life and activities much earlier than I should have done, throwing myself into the Christmas activities at the Y.W.C.A. When I went to church, I sat in the back row and tears ran down my face as I listened to the choir singing the beautiful anthems. The sermons contained nothing to heal my wounded spirit so I stopped going, and went to some Quaker meetings. Here again, the God of whom they spoke seemed so far away. Although I admired their good works, especially their pacifism, I felt that something was missing.

Sickened by the war and the sorrow it caused, I wondered if God had any interest in what was happening in this world. Tired out as I was at night, I tried to read a little from the New Testament. I read the words of Jesus, "Love one another." With all the accumulation of hate that was being poured forth, would it ever be possible for people to forgive one another? It seemed an impossible idealism for which to hope.

My boyfriend returned from Canada a fully-trained bomber pilot. He was due for leave and wanted me to spend a few days with him at his parents' home in Canterbury. We hadn't seen each other for six months, and as we walked in the woods and talked of the future we hoped to spend together, should we survive the war, I found that we had both changed and that our outlook on life differed radically. We seemed to have little in common. When I mentioned this to him and expressed my doubt as to whether we could enjoy a life together, he said that if it didn't work out we could always get a divorce. His remark stunned me! Remembering my own childhood, blighted by the breakdown in my parents' marriage, I knew I couldn't consider a union with Roy under these conditions. As my train left the platform, and Roy sadly waved to me, I knew we had seen each other for the last time.

The situation at home was not improving. My stepmother and I had nothing in common and my likeness to my mother aggravated her. Her jealousy was inevitable. I decided to move out and went to live in a Y.W. residential club. Once settled in I threw myself into the Christmas activities.

One night we had a dance at the Y.W.C.A. I liked to dance and went along in anticipation of having a good time. As usual, as part of my duties as a volunteer hostess, I circulated among the latest batches of men from the Forces. I was happy to have this position, as it gave me an excuse to not give too much attention to any one man. While the war was on I was afraid to let any one get too close to me again.

Halfway through the evening, I went to a quiet reading-room to be alone and rest awhile. Suddenly it was as though scales fell from my eyes, and I saw these young people around me as they really were - not gaily enjoying themselves but blasé and dissatisfied, trying to get something out of the motions they were going through yet bored with life. I felt that I no longer belonged, and left as soon as I could find an escort to take me home. The Christmas celebrations seemed so unreal - how could they sing "peace on earth and good will to all men", while this terrible carnage persisted! Where was God anyway, to allow it all to continue?

My enjoyment in my visits to ballet, opera, and concerts ceased to satisfy me. Time went by and periodically news of the death of several of my friends would reach me. One was killed in France, another at sea, while yet another died as his bomber crashed into the white cliffs of Dover, due to its failure to make the necessary height as it returned from a raid over Germany. One young man, a brilliant organist, was shot down in his plane. I felt I couldn't bear to entertain at the Y.W. anymore. Was this all we had to offer young me so soon to die?

How lonely I felt. How disillusioned! The voluntary work that I did at the club taught me that there is not more thankless a task than to work to please people. Human nature is so selfish and ungrateful. My strength was ebbing, and I felt I couldn't go on much longer. I cried to God to help me. Then Easter came.

FOUR

"DISILLUSIONMENT, DESPAIR, AND NEW BEGINNINGS"

We had four days of vacation for Easter and I longed to get away from London - where could I go? Then I remembered my guardians and knew they would be going to their house in the country. A wave of nostalgia swept over me, and I knew I must accompany them. Four days in the country listening to the skylarks as they soared into the sky; fetching the milk in the afternoons from the farm where the cows were handmilked - the idyllic country scenes passed through my mind as I considered the prospect.

My aunts welcomed me cheerfully, and the elder remarked that I looked as though I was in need of Mabel's good cooking! That night I literally collapsed into bed. The next morning I just couldn't get up and I was told to stay in bed as long as I liked. Sunday came and I was unable to move. Aunty Dukes (the elder) came and looked at me and took my pulse. She then went and told her daughter that they must call the doctor. He duly arrived and after examining me and hearing my medical history, he prescribed certain medicines and gave instructions that I remain in bed until he give me permission to get up. He said he would return when he had received my medical notes from London.

Three weeks passed and the doctor gave me permission to get up, but he stipulated that I remain at home for a few months, have plenty of rest, fresh air, and good food. I felt too weary to protest. The aunts phoned my father and work-place to give them the latest bulletin on my health.

Father insisted that I return to London to be examined by his doctor. Wanting to see the secretary at the Y.W.C.A. and my employer, to explain the situation, I agreed to go to London for the day, accompanied by Mabel.

My father's doctor confirmed the country doctor's assessment of my needs and gravely told Dad that if I did not have the care prescribed he would not be responsible for the outcome. My father, always having resented the appointment by my mother of her friends as guardians, fumed but had to let me go back to Fyfield.

How happy I was to leave London, though sad that my father had been so opposed to my staying in my guardians' home, even though I was in such need. My mother had known my stepmother, and had realized that, not being fond of children, she would not have given me a very happy childhood, hence the guardians. Aunty Phil, as I called her, took good care of my father but she certainly had resented my presence. She had succeeded in hiding her true feelings toward me from him. I would have dearly liked to have had her affection and had done my best to try to earn it without success. Jealousy is truly as cruel as the grave, as Solomon said. I didn't realize that this was the problem until later.

The doctor came on his customary visit. My aunts had returned to town and Mabel and I were alone. The doctor drew up a chair to have a chat with me. His words came as a shock - "You have had too strong an amount of radiotherapy, I'm afraid, and it's going to take a long while for you to recover from it and regain strength. You must reconcile yourself to a quiet life, no excitement and very light work when and as you are able to do it. You can't expect to return to a completely normal life for a very long time. It is a good thing that your aunts are able to have you here for an indefinite period and that you have Mabel to take care of you. I'll come in from time to time to see how you are getting along, but there is nothing more I can do to help you. Make the best of your stay here." He then left me, while I sat, stunned, on the couch.

Mabel came in with our 'elevenses'. I had heard the doctor talking to her in the hall, and knew that he had told her of my future prospects. I drank my coffee in silence, my thoughts in a whirl, and

Mabel sat quietly, knowing I had to have time to digest the words of the doctor. She took our cups and went into the kitchen.

The coffee revived me somewhat and after a little while, some of my natural optimism returned. Surely things were not as bad as the doctor had made out! I decided indeed to make the best of the situation. Unfortunately, the radio was out of order and I had not had time to get some good books together. However, for a time I was content just to lie and relax, lulled by the country sounds coming through the open windows. The war seemed so far away, with its air-raid sirens, bombing raids, ambulance and fire engines rushing through the streets. It was amazing how life went on in spite of it all.

My mind went back over the past few months. I remembered the afternoons when I had returned home, only to have to seek a place to pass between the bomb-craters or cope with roads blocked off because of the rubble piled up from bombed buildings. Miraculously, our eleven story building was still intact. On one occasion, it was discovered that an unexploded bomb had penetrated an apartment beneath us, but it was soon rendered harmless and removed by the courageous bomb disposal squad.

Lying there in the sun-filled room, it all seemed like a bad dream. I wondered how so many of us had managed to stay alive! As I considered the many escapes from death or injury that I myself had had, it humbled me. Why had I been spared when so many had been killed or maimed? Was there a God watching over me? My mind went instinctively to my grandparents. I knew that they were praying for us. Many mornings I had heard my grandfather praying as I passed his bedroom door. Often I had had the feeling that grandma was praying when she sat so quietly resting in her armchair with her eyes shut. Did prayer really work? On the other hand, perhaps it was just an impersonal fate that kept you until your time came around to die, as my father said. Either way, what happened after death? I began to feel uncomfortable. Was there a heaven and a hell? I'd been around so many people who didn't believe in either that I hadn't thought about it for a long time. I had a friend whose mother was the widow of a vicar, and a Spiritualist, and she didn't believe in hell. She was a gentle, cultured lady, and had invited me on several occasions to go with her to séances, as she was enthusiastic for me to make contact with my dead mother. It was a strong inducement and the idea fascinated me, especially as healings took place in some of the meetings. Maybe my voice could be restored! Strangely enough, however, each time I had arranged to go, something had prevented me.

Would the war ever finish? I had dabbled in politics, listening to the policies of all parties, including those of the communists. We used to discuss the sort of world we would like to have after the war. I realized by this time that it didn't depend so much on which party got in, as on the people who made up our society! My small experience had already shown me that people are basically selfish and that self-preservation was the only motivation that made them work together.

I sighed. My own problems were enough for me to face without taking on burdens of the world. I asked myself what sort of future was in store for me? I was afraid to get married in case it didn't work out. Where would I go and what would I do? My thoughts tired me and I went to sleep.

The next day I looked for something to read, to escape my thoughts. The only reading matter I could find were ancient bound editions of the Sunday School Magazine, published at the beginning of the century. When Mabel came in with our elevenses, I asked her if there was anything else in the house to read. She smiled and said that there was a Bible, if I would like to read that. I was going to refuse her offer when the thought struck me that it might be a good idea, after all, and asked her to bring it to me. She was pleased, I could see, but she made no comment. A dear soul, Mabel, I mused. She certainly looked after me like a mother and I was getting to know her, since my aunts had left. She didn't go to the Church of England but to a small Gospel Hall.

I started reading the Bible and worked my way through it until

I got to the book of Leviticus. There I gave up and told Mabel I'd had enough - it seemed so boring. She suggested I move on to the New Testament, which I agreed to do, and I discovered that I quite enjoyed the Gospel of Saint Matthew.

That night I found myself thinking over what I'd read about Jesus. His words were at the same time comforting and disturbing. If it were true that He had risen from the dead, what was He doing now? Could He really help people in these present days?

Looking back over the past four years since I had left my grandparent's home, I realized I had been very self-willed. Rejecting their way of life, I had put myself out on a limb, as it were, rejecting God. I hadn't found Him in the Methodist church, where no one had been interested in helping me when I had shown the desire to have Him in my life. Being christened and confirmed in the Church of England while in the choir had disappointed me. When the Bishop had laid his hands on me, nothing had happened and I felt no better afterwards. Neither could I relate to the Quakers, and their teachings didn't help me either. A few months earlier I had told my grandfather of my religious experiments, not wanting him to think that I had become completely pagan. He listened to me and then made one comment. Taking up his Bible he said, "Here is the only Book that will give you the Truth."

Well, here I was reading the Bible. But there were still so many questions in my mind. However, I continued reading through the Gospels, and the words of Jesus started working upon me. I couldn't stop reading. I felt God had me in a corner and I couldn't get out. He was making me face up to reality. All that I had been, all that I had done or failed to do, came before me. I squirmed as I lay there in bed.

I had been moving in the society of sophisticated, worldly people who were so often motivated by personal ambition even in wartime. Many of my contemporaries had adopted the motto: "Eat, drink, and be merry, for tomorrow we die!" I couldn't identify with them. When I was tempted to lower my standards in order to become one of the crowd, the memory of my grandmother checked me. The fight to hold my own against the tide of popular thinking and living drained me of my strength. I found that I wasn't only fighting outside influences but inner ones too. So much in me drew me towards things I didn't want to do. Later as I read the letter of the Romans, I could identify with Paul as he wrote: "For I know that in me, that is in the flesh (my lower nature), dwelleth no good thing" (see Romans 7:18).

Was God giving me another chance? I had a feeling that it might be my last. He had never let go of me, but had allowed me to go my own way. I had now truly come to the end of myself in more ways than one! The philosophies and other religions I had looked into had nothing to offer me and could do nothing for me now. Tears ran down my cheeks.

The story of the Prodigal Son came to my mind. Oh, this prodigal daughter was certainly eating the husks - husks of disappointment and disillusionment, of bitterness at wasted opportunities and talents. What was my life worth? Nothing! I couldn't even offer myself to God as a servant like the prodigal son had done to his father!

"Oh, Jesus!" I cried, "If you are really alive, please help me to know you. Teach me your Way and give me strength to walk in it. Take what is left of my life - I've made such a mess of it!" A quietness came over me. This time I had really surrendered to Jesus - there was no more fight left in me. I fell asleep.

When I awoke the next morning my mind immediately went back to the previous evening and the momentous decision I had made. Doubts assailed me - I believed in Jesus but there were still so many unanswered questions. Was the experience real? Had Jesus heard me and would He really give me the abundant life He had talked about in St. John's Gospel? A verse had hit me: "I am come that you might have life and have it more abundantly." What sort of life did He mean? I knew that it would rule out the feverish running around from one pleasure to another that had become part of my life, but that was out, anyway, since I was now an invalid. That was the negative side but I wanted something positive. Of course, I would now go to heaven, I supposed, when I died, but what about the here and now? I started reading my Bible again, looking for assurance that Jesus would do for me what He said He would do for those who put their trust in Him.

Mabel sensed the change in my attitude and came and sat on my bed. I started asking questions about the Bible and Jesus. Being the simple soul she was, Mabel couldn't give me the answers I needed. However she told me of a friend who lived nearby who would be pleased to visit and help me with my problems. How well the Lord had arranged things! I discovered that the friend was a Bible scholar, well known as a teacher in Brethren circles. Courteously he answered some of my intellectual questions about the Bible. Then, discovering my spiritual need he ministered to me from the Bible.

There and then the foundation had been laid for my future life with the Lord - squarely on His Word. I was shown that, according to Romans 8:15, I was now a child of God, born of His Spirit, who had come into my heart when I surrendered my life to Jesus. The marvelous third Person of the Holy Trinity would now teach and guide me, (John 16:13) and enable me to live the Christian life. I could count on this continual presence with me and the vigilance of angels over me. During the following six months I was guided in my study of the Bible by my new found friend, Mr. Adlam. He was a horticulturist as well as a Bible teacher, and I would sit on a box in one of his greenhouses and ply him with questions as he worked.

FIVE

"YOU SHALL RECEIVE POWER..." ACTS 1:8

For six months I remained at Fyfield. Mabel had been a true friend to me and my health was much improved. I appreciated my aunts' kindness in enabling me to stay in their home. My Bible teacher friend had been a spiritual father to me. I had spent hours with him, either in one of his large greenhouses sitting among the tomatoes or in our living-room, while he taught me from the Word.

During this time I received letters and visits from some of my friends, asking me not to get too religious. A youth leader from the Quakers travelled miles to suggest I take up healthy country pursuits and give up this intensive Bible study. A special boyfriend came down from London to find out what was happening to me. He was a reporter for a large newspaper and also a poet. I tried to "convert" him, but he wouldn't commit his life to Jesus. When I told him we would have to end our friendship, he sadly left me and joined the Air Force. I felt very bad about that. The failure of my efforts to produce a spiritual awakening in John and other friends left me very depressed. My spiritual father showed me that this had to be the work of the Holy Spirit. However, I felt sad at losing so many friends. Again I was told that we must learn to walk with Jesus in obedience and trust Him whatever happened. He would give me new friends.

While still convalescing, I left Fyfield to live with other relatives, at their insistence. After about a year I was allowed to do work for half a day. Six months later I was able to work full time. Two years after my conversion I was again living with my grandparents. My whole family now knew I was a changed person, but were all concerned because they thought I had become too religious! I witnessed to all of the transforming power of Jesus, yet I felt I still lacked something. I somehow couldn't get others to understand the Gospel. I was tongue-tied.

While reading in the book of Acts about the day of Pentecost and ensuing experiences I fell to wondering why the Christians I knew seemed so powerless today. Paul's first letter to the Corinthians, where he talks about the Gifts of the Holy Spirit, gave me much to think about. What meetings they must have had in those early days! I mentioned my queries to some of the elders at the Brethren Assembly I attended. The Gifts of the Holy Spirit were not for today, I was told. They were only for the early church.

At this time I met with two Christians who told me that believers did still have the Gifts of the Spirit. I went to their church and heard some of them in operation! I was thrilled and went back to my Assembly to tell my friends what I had seen. What a storm broke over my head! Books were given me telling of the satanic origin of experiences in a certain sect. I was confused and afraid, but not satisfied, and I searched in my Bible for the answer.

For a while I continued to visit the Pentecostals, as my new found friends were called, in between my own Assembly meetings. However, I was being regarded with suspicion in that quarter, so I no longer felt welcome there. Then I hurt my leg and had to stay home for two weeks, so I was unable to go to any meetings. I realized that this situation had been allowed by the Lord so I could settle the question once and for all! I reminded Him that He had promised to guide us into all truth, and then settled down to read His Word.

I remembered an experience I'd had while still in Birmingham. As I was on my knees reading the Psalms one morning, praise to the Lord welled up in my heart and I became full of joy. I had to get on my feet and express it somehow, but didn't know whether to laugh or cry! After a while this intense feeling subsided but I realized that something had happened to me that raised me to a new spiritual level. Thinking back on that beautiful experience, I wondered if it was the Baptism in the Spirit that I had received, but I hadn't spoken in "tongues", which was the outward sign of receiving this experience, as I had been led to believe.

Easter was at hand, and I went to a Conference in London. The morning meeting was inspiring and afterwards I went to a small room with others to wait upon God. As I knelt there worshipping Him, a sister came and laid her hands lightly upon my head.

Once again I was overwhelmed with joy and love, and I seemed to hear heavenly choirs. As I opened my mouth to find utterance, I found myself speaking in a language I had never learned. After a while it was time to go to the afternoon meeting, and still quietly praising the Lord, I sat down in the hall.

The members of an interdenominational Full Gospel Fellowship I sometimes visited, were holding their usual open-air meeting in Hyde Park that evening and I decided to join them. The words, "and ye shall receive power, after the Holy Spirit has come upon you," came into my mind. This would be the acid test of my experience, I thought. Until this time, partly due to my damaged vocal chords, I had been a very quiet speaker. I had been told that I would never make a preacher. However, as I stood in the circle that evening I felt the Spirit of God moving within me and I caught the eye of the leader. He nodded to me, and I moved into the centre of the circle and started speaking. At first it was my usual quiet voice but as the anointing of God came upon me, and I was moved by the need of those around me, my voice rang out over the crowd. People came over to listen and as I stopped, our leader moved in to ask those who were interested to come back with us to the church. Several gave their lives to the Lord that night. Surely I had proved the Lord yet again as I had trusted His Word - He would give me words and wisdom... Luke 21:15.

While seeking the Lord for the truth concerning the Baptism of the Holy Spirit, He made me realize that this experience was given to prepare one for service, not just to give an ecstatic 'trip'.

How far was I committed to serve the Lord, I asked myself? Would I leave all to follow Him? It was all right being a witness in my home town or in London, but what about the 'ends of the earth'? Well, I thought, I needn't worry about that - I was not strong enough to be a missionary. However, I did tell the Lord I was willing for whatever He wanted me to do.

It was not easy, being a member of a tiny independent Pentecostal Fellowship. The Brethren did have a certain prestige, as did the Salvation Army, but at that time the Pentecostals were treated as outcasts by other Christians and unbelievers alike. My family were upset and friends who lived in the same pleasant residential area avoided me. My old school friends made me feel that I had 'let the school down'. I didn't even fit into the Pentecostals very well - they were from the other side of town, except for my two new friends, who were much older than me. I tried to accept my situation without complaint, knowing that all of our circumstances are ordered of the Lord, but I felt hurt. Knowing that Jesus was also despised and rejected by His own, soothed my troubled spirit, however.

One day I invited an elderly street singer - a rarity in our area - into our home and gave him some food - He looked so tired. That got me into trouble with my eldest aunt. "Why don't you join the Army if you want to start a soup kitchen?" she remarked sarcastically. Grandmother soothed her down and renewed her efforts to get me into the Salvation Army. However, as much as I respected the great work done by that organization, and would have liked to please my grandparents, I could not do so because of some of the fundamental doctrines of the Bible which had been supplanted by their own military-style regulations. However, Mrs. Catherine Booth and her daughter, the Maréchal, have always been my heroines.

As I considered the large denominations, I felt sad, when I realized how far they had diverted from the original principles and ideals of their founders. There were so many good people in all of them and yet they were so divided. God had put a love in my heart for all of His people and I hated the barriers that separated them. We could all learn so much from each other.

SIX

"THE ANGEL OF THE LORD ENCAMPS AROUND THOSE WHO FEAR HIM" PSALM 34:7

The government started rounding up all available women to work in ammunition factories. I refused to go to help make bombs, knowing the carnage they caused, or to work in the offices connected to the factories, although they made me some tempting offers. The Labour Exchange did not know what to do with me. I wasn't strong enough to do nursing, even in the children's hospital. The Matron of The Great Ormond Street Hospital told me to come back in about a year's time. My doctor suggested the Land Army as it might 'toughen me up', so I agreed to apply.

On the morning that I was to be interviewed, I was led to read the following verse from the Bible: "a woman shall not wear men's clothing," Deuteronomy 22:5. I meditated on this and felt that it was a directive as to what I was to say to the Land Army Committee. This group of pleasant faced middle-aged women asked why I wanted to join. I was frank and told them of my objecting to making ammunition and willingness to do any other type of work. However, I would only accept an occupation that didn't require me to wear trousers. The ladies looked at each other, nonplussed, and one of them said that I could probably work on a poultry farm. Another asked me why I wouldn't wear trousers and that opened the door for me to testify. They then gave me a form to be filled in by my doctor. Two of the ladies, who both lived near me, then asked me round to have a cup of coffee with them in a couple of days' time.

When I went to see the doctor he was away and a lady locum

was taking his place. She read my medical notes and refused to sign the Land Army Form. Evidently, this would have entitled them to put me to digging ditches, should this be required. One would have no choice as to the type of work one would do! I thanked the Lord that He had caused my own doctor to be away. Surely the angels were watching over every detail of my life.

I was then sent to do light domestic work, part time, in the local hospital, where two of my old school acquaintances were nursing sisters! At first I worked with the Home Sister, whom I discovered to be a Jewess. I was careful in our conversation, when I spoke about Jesus and His claims to be the Messiah, but she soon had me transferred to other work. As I mixed with the other maids, some of whom had come from orphanages or very poor homes I learned about a side of life with which I had never had contact. However, after six months in the hospital, my doctor had me released from work there, as the tasks given me were too hard on my health.

While still at the hospital, I had an experience that impressed me greatly. The air-raids had become less frequent in London, so I occasionally went up there to stay with friends for the weekend in order to be able to attend a church called Peniel Chapel, in North Kensington. This was an independent Full Gospel Fellowship with over four hundred members. It was a lively congregation with a very full program and wide missionary involvement.

This particular weekend I spent the night at a friend's home, as usual. My bed was directly under a deep window. During the night, I was awakened by the scream of a bomb and jumped up, my nerves quivering. As the bomb landed, I called out "Jesus!" The blast shattered the window but it was as if a garden 'cloche' had been placed over me - I felt calm and at peace immediately. Instead of the glass from the window piercing my body, it had fallen on the ground outside! How great is our God and how great is His love! Again His angels had preserved my life.

Once more I returned to the Labour Exchange and wondered

what I would be sent to do next. The clerk was in a good mood and cheerfully said that she thought they'd got the right job for me at last! A vacancy had come up in a corrective home for delinquent girls, where an assistant was needed to help care for and supervise sixty girls between the ages of six and sixteen. The place was on the edge of town but I would have to live in, having two days off every ten days.

I was met at the Home by the Director, who showed me round and told me what my duties would be, also introducing me to other members of the staff. They were all quite a bit older than me and I wasn't very drawn to any of them, but I liked the Director who proved to be of Scottish descent and a Presbyterian. She was very frank with me, describing the situation which presented a real challenge. It appeared that the previous assistant had left the girls completely to their own devices in their free time. The result was that all the older ones spent this time in 'jitterbugging' - a form of so-called dancing that was very popular at the time. The modern word for it would be jiving I think!

The Director was unhappy about it but none of the staff would bother about organizing alternative activities. I said I would make this a priority if I took the post, and asked if she would give me a free hand to do what I thought best. The Director said that she hoped I would join the staff and that I could be sure of her support. She acknowledged that I was rather young for the post but felt it would be an advantage.

After prayerful consideration I decided that this position was truly the provision of the Lord, and that even the months of domestic work in the hospital had helped prepare me for it. My duties were wide-ranging, and I was given a huge bunch of keys and told that nobody was allowed to open a cupboard without the presence of a member of staff.

The day began by overseeing the dressing of the younger children. Then I had to line up those who complained of any type of ailment and decide who should see a doctor or go to sick bay, which was also under my care. Once the younger ones - those under fourteen - had left for school, I had to see that the older ones were formed into teams to do the chores of the Home. Each group did the cleaning, laundry and preparation of meals. A member of staff directed the work of each of these teams, and I had to take the place of the one who was off duty. I liked the cooking duty best - the girls were well trained and produced good meals, teaching me quite a bit about that art, I must admit!

The staff had their own dining-room but took turns to sit with the girls. The tables were set round three sides of a raised dais, on which there was a small table for the member of staff. One could therefore keep one's eye on the behavior of the children. I was dreading my turn at this duty!

All went well, for a few weeks, then one day, half-way through the meal, an argument started among the girls. Tempers flared and someone threw something at another girl. Mayhem ensued, with the girls shouting and throwing bread and cutlery at one another. I didn't know what to do so just bowed my head and prayed. After a few seconds - it seemed much longer - the noise stopped. I raised my head and saw all the girls staring at me. Several of the staff rushed in but I told them that everything was under control. They looked in unbelief at me, shouted some threats to the girls and left the room. I told the girls to clear up the mess or they would have no dessert and in a state of shock they did what I asked. There was no more trouble during my dinner-duty after that!

I had two hours off duty in the afternoon and was ready for a rest. However a door in my room opened out on to a fire escape. When I had been there a few weeks, some of the girls would sneak up the stairs and knock on my door, asking to speak to me. It seemed that I was the only believer on the staff. The others, bar the Director, were anti-religious - hardened by years of institutional life. They looked on me with some suspicion and a little mockery. The girls were not all there for faults of their own - many had come from homes cursed by alcoholism or a criminal parent. Some were more sinned against than sinners. Seeing my sympathy and care, these poor youngsters did all they could to spend time with me, even feigning to be ill to get into sick bay. I always fussed over the poorly ones a little, giving them Bible story books to read and extra hot drinks. My morning 'sick' queues got longer and longer until the Director came to my rescue and gave the girls a strict talking to. I valued the little time I was able to give the sick ones, however, as I was able to tell them about Jesus.

I had unearthed table games and a small library of books, and got some of the girls interested in these. However, although I cut the jitterbugging down gradually, introducing some square dancing, I got into the bad books of some of the older girls.

When bed time came I took the young ones down to the air-raid shelters to sleep. There wasn't enough space for them all so the older ones had to sleep in the dormitories. I made it my custom to pray for the girls in each shelter and dormitory, asking for the Lord's protection over them and many of the girls laughed at me. A staff member said, within the hearing of some of the girls, "Miss Kemp, it's no good praying for that lot!" Something happened to change their attitudes, however.

One night a bomb landed behind the Home. What had happened to me in London, now occurred here. Instead of glass in the windows shattering across the dorms, the glass fell outward. The girls were very subdued the next morning and treated me with respect from then on. Even the members of staff stopped making derogatory remarks.

Life was hectic and sometimes a girl would run away, adding to the stress of our work. On the weekends, the fire-escape was full of girls awaiting their turn to spend a few minutes with me. I didn't have the heart to turn them away but began to feel the strain of maintaining vigilance over all the activities of these young girls, many of whom had learned so much deception and wrong-doing in so few years.

Some of them accepted Jesus as their Saviour but I didn't have the time and opportunity to give them the spiritual nurture they needed. I could only commit them to the Good Shepherd who would send His angels to keep them in the often unsavory and temptation-laden environment to which they would later be released.

I was too tired to pray at night, and could only do so spasmodically while on my feet. I was rarely able to get to a meeting and began to feel drained spiritually, emotionally and physically. I couldn't carry on much longer. Finally, after fifteen months, I had to hand in my resignation. The Director said she would get some students in to help and tried to persuade me to stay. The girls were shattered and if I hadn't been so worn out I could not have resisted their pleas for me to stay. Feeling guilty and sad, I escaped as soon as I could to rest at my grandparents' home before getting another job. The memory of the girls haunted me for a long time.

SEVEN

"WHEN HE (GOD) OPENS NO ONE CAN SHUT"
REVELATION 3:7

I was then allowed to spend a year as a Mother's Help in a home just at the bottom of our road. The light work with two young children, in pleasant and tranquil surroundings, helped me to recuperate. The husband was Director of the Middle-Eastern section of the B.B.C. and fluent in Arabic. He was not very familiar with the Bible but more so with the Koran. He came from a strict Church of England family, however, and we had some interesting and hopefully fruitful discussions. Then came the end of the war and I felt that it was time to return to secretarial work.

Another two years passed uneventfully, during which time my grandfather passed on to his reward. I was able to help my grandmother, especially during the ensuing months, playing the old hymns to her that she loved, and taking her to and from the meetings at the Army.

By this time I had a job in the local government office, which was near home and situated in pleasant grounds. My chief was a Baptist and agreeable to work with, and he was interested in my taking exams in order to get promotion. I was enjoying good health, being much stronger. Nothing could have been better for me, but I wasn't happy. My thoughts were with the church in London that I had visited periodically. People from various denominations who had received the Baptism of the Holy Spirit congregated there to serve the Lord, with a true missionary vision. Several of the workers had gone to the mission field and were supported by the church. I yearned to belong to that church - was it just me, or was God trying to draw me there?

I had arranged to go up to London one weekend, and before I went I spoke to the Lord. "If you want me to go there and live and work, please see that I'm offered a job without having to look for it." I duly arrived at the apartment of my friend who was a midwife. She introduced me to another young woman who was staying with her. Elizabeth was married with two little children, and she talked a great deal about her husband, an engineer, who worked in a very worldly office. They both wished he could have a Christian secretary. Suddenly she turned to me and asked what sort of work I did. Now on my guard, I told her. "Wouldn't it be great if you could work for my husband!" she exclaimed. I replied that I lived out of London and was not seeking another job. The Holy Spirit reminded me of what I had asked the Lord earlier, however. So when she asked if I would be willing to go for an interview, I had to agree and gave her my address. Within two weeks I was offered the job by Ray, the engineer!

I broke the news to my family who began to raise objections. Uncle said it was virtually impossible to find accommodation in London so soon after the end of the war. Then the question of my health came up. I was well cared for at home and therefore much better but how would I fare in London, with the polluted air and having to take care of myself? Everything was done for me here and I could rest and relax after leaving the office. Life would be much more strenuous in London - was my health up to it? I couldn't answer, I only knew that the Lord had performed a small miracle to show me that He wanted me in London. The family was not convinced. "You'll be back soon," they commented, and shrugged their shoulders.

A young woman in the church was due to have her second baby at home, but the person who was going to stay with the family to care for them at the time, was unable to come. Hearing of this, I cancelled the holiday I had decided to take, and volunteered to care for the Lewises instead. My time with them was fully taken up and I had no opportunity to go flat hunting. Friends were concerned as to where I would go, when I left the family. I reminded them of a

Scripture that had always been precious to me, "Seek ye first the Kingdom of God and His righteousness and all these things (necessities of life) shall be added unto you." Matthew 6:33. My responsibility was to obey and leave the rest to Him.

Two days remained until I was obliged to leave the Lewises - they needed the room so I couldn't stay longer. "Dear Lord," I prayed, "please find me a place right away. My new job starts in three days' time. I'm trusting in You." I went to the open-air meeting, as usual, where I had become a regular speaker. After the following meeting at the church, a young woman, a stranger to me, came over and inquired if I needed a place to live. I told her that I did urgently, and she invited me to go home with her to see the accommodation she had to offer. Of course having been chosen for me by the angels, it proved to be just what I wanted and I moved in.

Open air meetings, house-to-house visitation, children's work, hospital visitation, ministering on the Thames Embankment to the down-and-outs - my time was full. However, the situation at the office was deteriorating and the conversation sickened me. Ray wasn't standing up to it very well either. I wasn't happy with the way things were going, and decided to ask the Lord for another job.

Soon after this a friend drew my attention to an advertisement for a job with a Christian organization that published New Testaments and Scriptures in many different languages. I applied, stating my church affiliation and so forth, but was not accepted. A few days later, my friend asked me to go with her to a meeting, held by the same organization. At the end of the meeting an appeal was made by the Secretary for help in the offices. My friend nudged me, but I was not inclined to apply again. However, she insisted and I gave him my name and address, which strangely, he did not recognize. When I mentioned my previous application, he told me that he had heard nothing about it! After an interview, I was given the post, and later understood why I had been refused the first time - the gentleman who received my application did not agree with the doctrines of our church!

That was a real lesson to me - I learned that when God opens a door, no man can shut it, and vice versa. How happy I was - my new chief was a quiet man with a good sense of humour. When I presented myself on the first day in his office, he remarked, "I do hope you haven't received a call to the mission field. The last two young ladies who worked with me have both gone abroad!" I laughed and reassured him, telling him that I wasn't robust enough for the foreign field.

EIGHT

"LED BY THE SPIRIT OF GOD..." ROMANS 8:14

One Saturday evening, a friend and I met together but were uncertain as to what to do, as the open-air meeting had been cancelled. As we waited for the Lord to show us, the Thames Embankment Mission came to both of our minds. Sandwiches and tea were served there every night to the poor souls who had become the outcasts of society, after which a simple service was held. We helped in this ministry quite regularly, often listening to the stories of these ruined lives. One man had been an Oxford don but drink had been his downfall. In that place, overhung by the smell of disease-ridden, unwashed bodies, it was so satisfying to witness to a Lord who can save from the uttermost to the uttermost!

When Mair and I arrived at the Mission it was to find that, for a change, there were plenty of helpers. We left and were strolling along the embankment, wondering what the Lord wanted us to do. When we passed a seat, I noticed a man sitting there, looking so tired and lonely. I felt the inward nudge of the Spirit, and spoke to Mair, who had the witness that we should speak to him. We therefore retraced our steps and joined him on the seat. We discovered that he had walked up from the country looking for work but had found none. When we asked if he had eaten that day he rather hesitantly said that he hadn't. It was obvious that he was not a 'sponger' so we invited him to have a meal with us, and, again very hesitantly, he agreed. Gently pressing him for further information, we learned that he had nowhere to spend the night and no money. After the meal, we took him to our friends at the Embankment Mission and arranged for him to stay there the night. Before we left him he agreed to come to church with us the next day.

When we called to take him to church, we had a good talk enroute, and he asked us why we had done so much to help him. When we told him how the Lord had brought us to him, he was very moved. Then he told us that the previous evening he had been waiting by the river for nightfall, so that he could commit suicide. We were really shaken that this young man's life had depended on our obedience to the Holy Spirit. That evening, he accepted Jesus as his Saviour. We took him back to the Mission, where the kindly Director took over. We saw him from time to time and were so happy to learn that the Lord was undertaking for all his needs, and that he was also helping to minister to the needs of others.

As I had lain on my bed for a few minutes, on my night off, I felt a deep sense of satisfaction. Since I had come to London, fourteen months ago, I had put my heart and soul into serving the Lord in the various ministries to which He had led me. I had also become interested in helping to support a missionary who was working in the Congo.

This evening as I sat at my table, I was thinking of my friend in the Congo and was considering how much money I could send her, after putting aside my tithes and offerings to the church. How wonderful it must be to go and give all your time to ministering the Gospel to people who were really keen to hear it! Sadly, I considered the situation in England, where so few people were interested. In spite of all the work done, just one person here and there accepted the Good News. In Africa and elsewhere it was the other way round, with few labourers and so many ready to listen and accept Jesus and His love.

A voice penetrated my thoughts. I couldn't tell you now whether it was an audible voice or whether it came from the Holy Spirit within me, speaking to my heart. The voice said, "Why don't you go?" I sat quietly, awed. It was definitely the Lord who was speaking to me. "I'm not strong enough," I replied. Even as I spoke, I realized how foolishly I had answered! I knew that if He told me to go, I would go, regardless of any consideration. In His Word He had said that His strength was made perfect in weakness, so I didn't pursue the matter further. I just said, "Lord, where do you want me to go? Please show me how to start preparing."

I was due for two weeks' vacation and had made my plans at the insistence of a friend who had wanted me to go to Lynton in Devon. I realized that this break would give me time to wait on the Lord and receive more direction from Him. The Rev. Percy Parker and his wife ran a guesthouse for Christian workers. So, apart from the rest in beautiful surroundings, I would enjoy fellowship with God's people.

A few days after my arrival, Mr. Parker informed us that he was opening a Bible School there in three weeks' time. He had been the Principal of the Elim Bible College but had retired and now felt it was time for him to start a non-denominational school. The Holy Spirit spoke to me, "This is where you are to come."

I was enjoying the fellowship of several young people who were helping in the guesthouse while waiting for the school to open, and it was good to know that I would soon be joining them. At the end of my holiday, I just had time to return to London to work out my notice and bid good-bye to all my friends at the church.

I hated having to take my leave of the chief in the office, after what I had told him on my acceptance of the post! However, as a true Christian he graciously wished me well and told me that all of the staff would be praying for me. Happily, the Lord found him someone to take my place very quickly.

My relatives were shocked, and my father was angry. I had been in the habit of visiting him and my stepmother once a week. I had forgiven her for her behaviour that had forced me to leave home. They all made dire predictions as to what would happen to me. Even my brethren at the church were doubtful as to whether I was taking the right step. However, I knew that I had heard from the Lord, and that he was leading me. "God has chosen the foolish things of the world to shame the wise; God has chosen the weak things of the world to shame the strong..." 1 Cor. 1:27. Having arranged all of my affairs, I returned thankfully to Devon, just in time for the opening of the school.

NINE

"PREPARATION AND A PROPOSAL"

How I enjoyed the opportunity to study the Scriptures and in such a lovely environment. Surely the Lord was good to me! The hectic life in London had been a greater strain on my health than I had realized, and I was grateful for the country air and food with unhurried routine to build me up again. Now I just wanted confirmation as to which country I must go, as there was language study to think about. I had considered the Congo, as I had been thinking of that country when the Lord called me. Also, one of the girls at the school was going there, and I thought that perhaps we might be going together. However, I was disappointed when I saw her becoming friendly with one of the young men students. I waited on the Lord and Brazil started coming more and more to mind. I remembered the excerpts from newsletters from missionaries there, that a friend used to read to me. Other indications made it clear that Brazil was the land to which I was to go. Rather sadly, and a little fearfully, I accepted the fact that I might have to go alone. Alone? No, not alone. Surely to walk in obedience to my Lord, with all the assurance of His presence, should be enough for me! I wept before Him as I told Him that I was ready to go to Brazil if He so desired, and a sweet peace came into my heart. I said nothing of all this to any of my fellow-students and was glad that I didn't, as a little while later I found out that one of them, a young man called Gordon Emmens, was going to Brazil!

The term proceeded uneventfully. Several of us would go for long walks together, on the weekends. Gordon never accompanied us. He had come from a strict Bible College, where the men were forbidden to talk to the girls. He mildly disapproved of the mixing of the sexes in the informal atmosphere of this small school. Also, he was a confirmed bachelor, a real loner, impatient to finish his preparations to go to the mission field. We wondered, really, why he had come down to Lynton. We were soon to find out!

When on my own, I quietly thought about Brazil. I had heard sufficient about the situation in that country while in London, both from visiting missionaries and their newsletters. I shuddered at what I remembered, as I thought about the snakes and scorpions. and above all, the attitude of the Roman Catholics towards the Protestants. I knew they were fanatical wherever they were in power, going to all lengths to stop opposing activities. In Southern Ireland, kidnapping those of their number who became converted was quite a common occurrence. I had heard of the unpleasant things which had happened to missionaries who had dared to step on Catholic territory.

After class one day, which had dealt with demonology, we were discussing the subject of the powers of darkness and demons. Some of the students, who had been abroad during the war, related how they had felt the power of evil in certain places, especially where demon-worship was practiced. Gordon mentioned that he had felt it in a certain place near the school, where somebody had once committed suicide. I became interested and wanted to know the whereabouts of the place.

He volunteered to take me, to my surprise, and so early one evening, I accompanied him to a very beautiful little glade by the river. The actual place was so peaceful, under the shadow of the trees, and I leant on the side of a little rustic bridge that spanned the narrow river. "Maybe I'm not so sensitive to the atmosphere as you," I remarked. "This is a beautiful spot and I really don't sense any evil power here!" I forgot his answer because he then turned and looked me full in the eyes and said, "Jacqueline, I believe God has sent you to me to be my wife!" My first reaction was indignation, at the thought that he should have got me there under false pretences!

However, his quiet, steady look made me realize his sincerity. My mind was in turmoil and I hedged, "How do you know that God wants me to go to Brazil? For all you know He may have called me to the Congo!" Gordon remained calm and said that when he first saw me, while I was on holiday and not even a prospective student, God had told him that I was to be his wife! I lifted my heart to the Lord in bewilderment. "Lord, I thought you wanted me to remain single and go to Brazil alone. If this is really of you, please show me." I determined not to be affected by the romantic surroundings or to be rushed! In the past I had let my heart rule me and had only brought suffering upon myself as a consequence. This time I knew I must be cool-headed, especially as this was also to be a partnership in God's work. We walked home quietly, and I told Gordon that he must give me time to seek the Lord in the matter. I did tell him, however that I was called to Brazil, which really encouraged him!

We began spending time together and a certainty grew in my heart that the Lord had indeed brought us together. Finally we became engaged and six months later we were married! I would have liked to spend more time studying but Gordon was impatient to begin preparing to go to Brazil. We both got jobs in order to help us buy the necessary equipment.

My relatives, even more dismayed that I was going to Brazil, were a little more reconciled to the fact when they saw that the Lord had provided me with a strong, very practical husband. Even so, they thought that Gordon was foolhardy to marry me when there was little possibility of my passing the medical test!

Gordon had been brought up in a good home that was not, however, religious. Besides swimming, he had also enjoyed fishing and boating on the river at Southampton, which was his home town. He and his brothers had built their own boat and many were the escapades in which they had been involved! Coming from a very sheltered childhood - not even being allowed to go camping with the Girl Guides because of physical frailty, the tales of Gordon's boyhood days found a receptive ear. Having always enjoyed the

"William" books, "Tom Sawyer" and such like, I seemed to have found someone who embodied these adventurous spirits!

Gordon did not excel at school, which was not surprising. Although having the ability, he was too restive to apply himself. He had a problem with his eyesight which had been a hindrance but had provided him with a good excuse for getting by with a minimum of study!

For a while he was sent to Sunday School where, with his stink bombs and general mischievousness, he made life difficult for his teacher. What he heard there did not make much impression on him. Leaving school early, he decided to make hotel and catering work his career.

When World War II broke out he was only seventeen and a half, so he put his age up and volunteered for the Army. He was placed in the artillery, trained and sent to the front-line defence forts outside Portsmouth. Where the anti-aircraft guns had the grim work of trying to intercept and shoot down the enemy 'planes as they came over to bomb our country and of preventing enemy forces from invading.

TEN

One day, a gun-skidding fell on his foot, crushing it and breaking his big toe. He was sent to the hospital, where his foot was put into a light plaster cast. A few days later, he and a friend slid down the drainpipe and went to a tea-dance, where he was spotted by the Matron of the hospital, engaging in a tag-dance. The next day, the doctor noted that the cast on his foot was cracked and put on a heavy one, remarking that Gordon would not be able to dance in that!

In due time, he was sent to a camp to convalesce, where wounded men from all regiments went to recuperate and train in readiness to rejoin their units. While there, Gordon became very impressed by a young Guardsman who went up and down the lines of men as they queued for food, preaching to them from the Bible. Gordon admired his physique and his courage but let the earnest words spoken by the Guardsman go in one ear and out the other, his mind being too full of his own schemes to pay much attention. He and a friend in his barracks were already planning their future after the war, and there was no place in it for God, since they were aiming at obtaining and running a night-club in London. The friend later went on to achieve this, but when Gordon visited him to tell him the Good News, he told him curtly to get out!

At the end of his convalescence they were all given their back pay. Many spent their first evening out drinking, and Gordon was among them. Normally able to carry his drink well, this night he had to be picked up and carried to camp by a policeman who, as it happened, was a Christian. Before he left, he prayed for Gordon. The next afternoon, with no money in his pocket, Gordon sauntered round town, seeking amusement. It was Sunday and most places were shut. Bored, he saw over a shop window an announcement that tea and cakes were being served, free of charge, to members of His Majesty's Forces. He decided that, nothing stronger being available, he might as well have some tea, so he went in and sat down by himself at one of the tables. Soon a sweet-looking, elderly lady brought him a cup of tea, sandwiches and cakes. Sitting down beside him she quietly asked him if he knew Jesus Christ as his Saviour. Embarrassed, Gordon said, "That sort of thing is for good people, not men like me, ma'am." The lady pursued the subject telling him that, on the contrary Jesus loved him!

However he tried, Gordon was not able to deter her from telling him the Gospel and, in spite of himself, he couldn't help thinking about her words as he sat there sipping his tea. The thought that Jesus loved him gripped his heart and, there and then, the desire grew in him to respond to that love. An invitation was given to all present to stay for the evening meeting to be held there, and he remained. That night he received Jesus as his Saviour and was born again of the Holy Spirit. He knew that something had happened to him that night that had changed him completely! As he walked back to the barracks, joy filled his heart, and a peace. He was a new creature - "the old things had passed away and all things had become new". (11 Cor.5:17)

Soon afterwards he was sent back to his old unit. Advised to nail his colours to the mast right away, he knelt down by his bunk that night to pray. Rather to his surprise, no boots were thrown at him and silence reigned in the barracks. Of course, the men knew that Gunner Emmens could be a tough customer to take on in a fight, which no doubt deterred them! As he got up some remarked that he had 'gone religious'. Gordon told them then and there that he had asked Jesus Christ into his life. Nothing more was said that night but the men watched him day by day, laying bets as to how long his conversion would last. No one could persuade him to go out for a drink with the boys, as of old. Even the Church of England chaplain, who came up to him one day to invite him to go and have a beer with him, was refused. "You're taking this too far," was his comment.

The desire to smoke did not leave him so quickly. He had developed a smoker's cough, as he chain-smoked - the habit had him fast. Knowing it had no place in his new life, Gordon did his best to quit. He'd even tear up the cigarette he had already started smoking and throw it away, only to return and pick up the pieces! He felt that there was just no way to get free. Then, one day, about six months after his conversion, the thought came to him that Jesus was now Lord of his life - nobody or anything else should dominate him. Resolutely he threw his last cigarette away and left it there.

During this time, in spite of the smoking and the ensuing conviction that came upon him, he knew that the Lord was with him, and he enjoyed victory in other areas of his life.

One day, as he left a missionary meeting, he was gripped by the feeling that the Lord was calling him to be a missionary. He saw a vision of himself preaching to a crowd of brown-skinned people, and wondered who they were. That night he surrendered his life to the Lord, to go wherever he wanted him to serve.

Some time later he was walking along a street by the docks in Southampton, wondering to which country God was calling him. He saw a costermonger's cart by the pavement full of oranges and bought a couple. As he skinned one of them, his eye fell on the name printed on it in blue dye - Brazil. The Holy Spirit spoke to him, "That is where you are to go - Brazil."

ELEVEN

"A THREEFOLD CORD IS NOT EASILY BROKEN"
ECCL. 4:12

Gordon, like me, had many close encounters with death. Such was his trust in the Lord to keep him that his companions would often gather round him, however, when things were 'hot'. One night, while still on the Fort, he was manning an anti-aircraft gun when he had a strange experience. A raid was in progress and the enemy had succeeded in putting one gun at his side out of action. He managed to get an oncoming 'plane into his sights and fired. The gun jammed. As the 'plane dived right over him, its machine-gun rattling, Gordon flattened himself on the ground. When it had passed over he got up and rushed underground to check his gun, in order to find out why it had jammed. His comrades had taken shelter there and watched him take the gun to pieces. A bullet had jammed in the magazine - it had been badly packed. As his anger at having missed shooting down the 'plane subsided, he came to realize that, if the gun had fired the tracer bullets, their position would have been revealed to enemy 'planes coming in behind. An angel had certainly been involved in this incident!

Gordon had been posted to go overseas several times but on each occasion his name had been crossed from the list. He had volunteered - against his father's advice - for several dangerous missions - but was never accepted. His eldest brother's company had been wiped out and Alfred was the sole survivor. Still, Alfred was sent time and time again to the hottest areas of battle until finally, when nearing Paris, he was blown up and left exposed so long that he contracted pneumonia, which developed into TB. He was invalided out of the Army, wrecked in health and having lost his entire savings during the last battle. Gordon was spared all of this.

Now the war had ended and he was free to prepare himself for the Lord's service. After a while, he went to Bible College in Birkenhead where, with other ex-servicemen, he worked and studied and sought God. He was finding it hard going - the standards set seemed unattainable - when he met some believers who told him he needed the power of God in his life and should seek the Baptism of the Holy Spirit. He started seeking God with his whole heart, hungry for all that He would give him. One Sunday, while in a prayer-room in his home town, the Lord graciously baptized him with the Spirit and Gordon found that this truly opened up a new dimension in his spiritual life.

After leaving Birkenhead, he returned home for a time. Then he was told about Rev. Parker's place in Devon, and it was suggested that he go there. Gordon asked the Lord for a certain sum of money, as confirmation that he should go. One evening, at 6:55 p.m. precisely, he arrived at the home of a dear elderly lady whom he occasionally visited. She opened the door with a big welcoming smile. "Oh, Gordon, I am glad to see you!" she said. "I have been given a sum of money that I felt you should have and so I asked the Lord to send you along by 7:00 p.m. if he wanted you to have it." Gordon then told her about the sign that he had asked for, and they both praised God for His goodness. Within two days he had packed his things and started on the long cycle ride to Lynton.

The Lord graciously gave another sign that he was on the right track. The first evening he stopped at the home of an Army colleague, who had given him his address. His mother welcomed Gordon as her own son and said that for some reason or other she had prepared a meal for three instead of two! Angels had certainly gone ahead of him!

Gordon was not sure why the Lord had sent him to Lynton. However, when he saw me he knew! He had thought that he should remain single, as the rigors of missionary life would be too hard to expect a wife to share them. He bided his time until the opportunity came for him to get me by myself, as already recounted.

How wonderfully the Lord had brought us together. I am sure the angels must have enjoyed this particular mission.

TWELVE

"TRIALS AND CHALLENGES"

While we were living in a bedsitter in Southampton, working at secular jobs in order to buy our equipment, and so on, Gordon developed pneumonia. He became as weak as a baby and the doctor gravely took me to one side and said that he feared Gordon would never get to Brazil, as he was spitting blood. Some brethren came and prayed for him but nothing seemed to happen until, about three days afterwards. Gordon suddenly sat up, then got up and dressed. "I am healed," he said, and told me that he was going to the meeting at our church. I ran after him and cried, "You'll die, Gordon!" He didn't die however, and when the doctor came the next morning he was very surprised. "I insist on you having lung x-rays and seeing a specialist," he said, so Gordon complied with his wishes. After examining Gordon and the x-rays the specialist turned to Gordon and said, "Why are you wasting my time? There is nothing wrong with you!"

Then I became ill with jaundice and as soon as I was on the road to recovery we decided that we should give up our jobs and go back to Lynton. After a time of convalescing in Lynton and helping in the work, we were invited to Southern Ireland to hold an evangelistic campaign in the country. We had met people from all over England and had many invitations to visit and preach, but felt that we should first of all go to Ireland. The nursing sister, being one of those we had met in Lynton, made the arrangements for our visit and gave us instructions as to how to get to the place. We were to stay with her sister, and a local farmer was going to let us have a large barn in which to hold the meetings.

It was late September when we arrived at the simple farmhouse where we were to stay. Our sister did her cooking on an open fire in the middle of the kitchen-cum-living-room where chickens walked in and out. Neither of us had stayed before in so primitive a place. "Good training for Brazil" we whispered to each other. Our hostess was very welcoming and did her best for us. Her husband was a fanatical Catholic and had left her, but came to visit from time to time. She informed us that it was quite a while since his last visit.

The day after our arrival, we went to see the farmer to make arrangements about the meetings. The barn was full of wheat and he explained apologetically that we wouldn't be able to use it for quite a while! What were we to do? We couldn't wait around for an indefinite period until the barn was free - our hostess was poor and we hardly had any money to pay for our keep. Had we gone wrong somewhere and misunderstood the leading of the Holy Spirit?

Over supper that evening we were discussing the situation with our sister when a big, black-browed man walked in through the door. Our hostess visibly paled - it was her husband! He demanded to know who we were and what we were doing there. When we informed him he fell into a rage and ordered us out of the house immediately! It was nine o'clock at night and we looked at each other, dismayed. However, we quickly packed our bags and sadly took leave of our sister. The husband glared at us and if looks could kill, we should have died on the spot!

As we walked down the lane, we were aware that we were in the middle of the countryside, with just an isolated house here and there - not even a village in sight. There was a little light from the moon and, to our dismay, it started raining. "Oh, Gordon, what a start to our missionary career," I almost wept. "Cheer up Jackie, we know that the Lord brought us here - He will not let us down!" said Gordon.

We had trudged for about half a mile when we saw the lights of a house. Gordon knocked at the door and it opened a chink - a suspicious face peered out. Gordon asked if they had a room where we could sleep for the night, assuring them that we would pay for it. "Who are you and where do you come from?" he was asked. He explained. "You are Protestants?", the woman asked. "Yes we replied." "Then you can't come in here!" She shut the door in our faces with a bang. We walked on. The line of a hymn came to my mind - "God will take care of you!" We sang quietly as we covered another half a mile. How heavy my case had become! Another house came into sight and we stopped and prayed. Then we walked up to the door and knocked. This time a more friendly-looking man looked out at us. Again we asked if they could put us up for the night. He asked a few questions and, seemingly satisfied, invited us in.

We discovered that he and his wife were believers who had rather lost out in their relationship with the Lord, owing to lack of fellowship. How kind they were when they learned of our situation. We had a warm drink and then shared a Bible-reading and prayer with them before we went to the bed they prepared for us. Our hearts were full of thankfulness as we laid our heads down to sleep. The angels had indeed gone before us once again, and prepared the way.

The next morning we ate a delicious country breakfast, followed by a good time of fellowship with our hosts. They realized that the Lord had sent us along to reassure them of His care and continued presence with them. We all rejoiced together and our hosts renewed their commitment to Him.

What was to be our next step? It was Sunday and our host told us that no transport was available, urging us to stay. Gordon however, felt a sense of urgency in his spirit to make for Belfast and said we would hitch-hike and trust the Lord to provide transport to Londonderry, the nearest large town. Our brother therefore helped us carry our luggage to the nearest road, where he waited with us. After we had been waiting almost thirty minutes a small van came along. It stopped, and the driver asked us where we wanted to go. As it 'happened', he too, was going to Londonderry! "A miracle," whispered our brother as he helped put our bags in the back of the van.

On our arrival, we went straight to the railway station and discovered there was a train leaving for Belfast in about three hours' time. We found that a meeting was being held that afternoon in the Mission Hall, so we made our way there. While on our way, we asked the Lord to arrange for someone to take us back to tea afterwards, as we were hungry and had no money to spare for food.

Sure enough, after the meeting, a couple came and spoke to us and invited us to their home for a meal! We just had time to enjoy a lavish tea before hurrying to the station to catch our train. Our kind host took us there in his car. When I asked Gordon what we were going to do in Belfast, he told me that he had been given the address of a lady who lived there, and felt we should try to find her.

By the time we arrived in Belfast it was nearly eight o'clock and people were returning home from church. We made enquires as to which tram we should take and boarded the one indicated. It was full of passengers and Gordon had to stand. After a few minutes he bent down and whispered to me to speak to the ladies behind me, which I did. I found that they were Christians, on their way home from church. We asked them if they knew the address we had been given. It turned out that they knew the lady who lived there and volunteered to accompany us to the house. As we made our way there, we told them a little about our situation.

THIRTEEN

*"THE STEPS OF A RIGHTEOUS MAN ARE ORDERED
BY THE LORD" (PS 27:23)*

The house we were seeking was not far from the tram stop. Our new friends stayed at the gate while we knocked on the door. There was no answer. We stayed there for a few minutes, knocking again several times but there was still no response. My heart went down to my boots - what were we going to do now? Strangers in a strange land, without money to pay for a night's lodging! The two ladies patiently waiting looked at us. One of them, her kind, round face smiling, said in her Irish brogue, "Don't worry, the Lord has told me to take you home with me!"

We stayed with Ida for six weeks, during which time we made many other friends. Ida was known all over Belfast as a Gospel singer, and she opened doors for us to minister in a variety of churches and halls. How wonderfully the Lord had provided for us! Many of those we met became our prayer partners and helped us when we went to Brazil. Then we received a request to hold an evangelistic campaign in Portadown.

When we arrived there we found that there were only about seven or eight people in the church! Board and lodging was provided for us in a small boarding-house with a cafe. Our room was at the top of the three-story house. For several days we went from house to house, handing out invitations to the meetings. When there was no response, we decided to fast and pray.

I managed only three days, being unused to fasting, but Gordon continued for seven days. Every morning the tantalizing smell of eggs and bacon, his favourite meal, wafted up to our room, but he steadfastly resisted the temptation.

The situation changed and we were invited into some of the houses we visited. In one very poor home, we found that the wife was waiting for her husband to be released from jail, after serving a short sentence for theft. She came to the meeting and gave her life to Jesus, as did her little daughter. We prayed for her husband, Jimmy, and on his release from jail we took him out for a meal. He came to the meetings with his wife and daughter and within a few days he also accepted Jesus as his Saviour. It transpired that one of the objects he had stolen was a bicycle belonging to one of the elders of the church! One night, after the Holy Spirit had really moved in the hearts of the congregation, the bicycle owner embraced the thief as they both came down to the front, seeking the Lord for blessing!

How the Lord blessed those meeting! Within a short time the church was almost full. Several of the brethren wanted us to stay in Ireland and open a Revival Center. We knew we couldn't however - Brazil was calling us. Gordon had one more engagement to fulfill which he felt should be our last in Britain. He had been invited to Scotland for a campaign, but we were concerned about all the new converts we were leaving behind. Finally it was decided that I should remain behind to help teach them and establish the work.

I had felt the desire to do some midwifery, thinking it would be useful in Brazil, and the Lord now opened up a way for me to do this. I went to the local maternity home and found they had a vacancy for an auxiliary nurse. I was taken on and in this way I earned my living, learned a lot about midwifery and was able to help in the church. I was put on night-duty soon after, which meant I was able to give my evenings to teaching etc. Also, as most babies so often seem to arrive in the night and early morning, I got a lot of experience! The staff, all Catholics except for the Matron, were very kind and helpful to me, going out of their way to teach me all they could. After three months, Gordon having returned to Ireland, we went to Belfast. The staff at the maternity hospital predicted that I would be pregnant within a year! I laughed and told them we couldn't start a family yet.

However, they proved to be right!

While in Belfast, Gordon met a Baptist who was a dental surgeon at a big hospital and also a professor in charge of a dental college. He offered to teach Gordon basic dentistry, so that he would be able to extract teeth. Finding Gordon to be an apt pupil he said it was a pity Gordon couldn't take the whole training, as he was cut out for the work. His first patient in the hospital was an old lady whose teeth were almost falling out. He did the extractions so well and with such care that she enthused about the job he had done, saying she had never had a better dentist! At the end of Gordon's course, his doctor friend gave him a set of instruments, with his blessing. We then left Ireland, rather reluctantly, as we had grown to love the country and its people. However, Gordon had agreed to take one more campaign in Scotland, in a mining town.

We stayed in the home of a miner and his wife, Dan and Lizzie and their family. I soon got accustomed to being called 'hen' by our jovial host, and was made to feel at home with them. On the third day of the campaign, Gordon 'happened' to be out walking when he saw a little girl fall onto a spiked iron railing. He took her to the hospital and then contacted her family. Her father turned out to be one of the most notorious characters in the neighborhood, known for his hard drinking and gambling. His home contained only the bare necessities and his wife was a sad, poorly dressed woman. Jock Boyd was working down the mine, and so, after assuring the mother that her little girl was not seriously hurt, Gordon invited her to the meetings. She seemed afraid of her husband's reactions and would not commit herself. When Jock met Gordon later, he thanked him warmly for helping his little girl and asked what he could do to show his gratitude. Gordon promptly replied that he would like most of all for Jock to come to the meetings with his family.

That evening, the wife and children came alone. Then, just as the introductory singing was ending Jock came in, dead drunk, and staggered into a seat near the back. He roared out, "sing 'On the old rugged cross, will ye?" Gordon led the congregation in singing this and then Jock called out another hymn, which we also sang, after which Gordon preached. As he finished speaking, Jock called out, more subdued now, "Sing 'Just as I am, Without One Plea'." As we sang those beautiful words Jock stumbled up the aisle, fell on his knees and wept his way into the Kingdom of God. The next night his wife came forward, together with their children, his mother and sister. All found Jesus as their Saviour. How we rejoiced!

What an uproar there was in the mine - Jock Boyd had become a Christian! Bets were made as to how long he would last! The meetings came to an end and we left Harthill, to finish our preparations for our journey to Brazil. However, seven years later, during our furlough, we had the opportunity to visit that town again, and had a meal with Jock Boyd and his family. What a transformation, both in him, his family and his home! Carpets now covered the floor and nice furniture filled the house. His wife and children were nicely dressed, but best of all, as a Christian family they showed the love and joy on their faces that only Jesus can give!

FOURTEEN

DEPARTURE, ARRIVAL, AND A BAD START

The money for our fares had come in. We had spent a year itinerating and holding the three campaigns. Contacts made at Lynton had opened doors for us and given us prayer partners in many parts of Britain. Our hearts overflowed with gratitude as we looked back and saw how the Lord had paved the way for us. Surely the angels had been there, smoothing our path.

We made our final purchases, in which were included a bee-keeper's hat (which I thought might help to keep out the mosquitoes), and a pair of women's army boots which laced up over my ankles. I was wearing a pretty full-skirted summer dress when I tried them on and Gordon roared with laughter - what a sight I looked! In our boxes were a pressure-cooker, two storm lamps, two camp beds and a small camouflaged army tent. All these were carefully packed together with our wedding presents in solid trunks dug out from dusty recesses in Southampton's second-hand shops.

Gordon and I had decided to go to Brazil under the auspices of the Gospel to Brazil Faith Mission. This undenominational Full Gospel Mission had been founded in 1938 by a brother named Albert Mundy and his wife Dora. They had commenced a work in Patos, in the interior of Paraiba, spreading out to various outstations. This couple who were from Southampton, were supported by Gordon's church. They had been joined by another couple and a single young man about two years previously. These missionaries had moved out into other areas, even as we expected to, after a time of language study and orientation into the work by the Mundys. Their work had grown and is continuing unto this day, being developed by the Medcrafts. No income was provided - we had to trust the Lord to send money for our needs, from those whose hearts were touched.

The great day came and we were given a quiet send-off by some friends in Liverpool. We travelled in a Booth Line Mail Boat, together with another missionary couple and a single lady. The sea remained calm (it was early August), and the journey was a pleasant one. Our Captain, who was a very agreeable man, allowed us to take a turn at the wheel and showed the resulting zigzag on the chart! He also showed us the marvels of radar and other instruments on the bridge.

We'd been at sea for two weeks when we arrived at a small port in Northern Brazil, where we spent half a day. Full of excitement, Gordon and I went on to the shore and walked along the clean, unspoiled beach. Several one-story houses were set back behind a narrow road, running alongside the beach, with palm trees providing a fitting background. Suddenly rain fell! 'Fell' is the correct word- it was as though some heavenly sluice-gates had been opened! Within a minute we were soaked to the skin, and turned to run back to the ship. Then a young man came out of one of the houses and beckoned to us. We ran towards him and he pulled us into the house.

We had tried to learn some Portuguese but were not equal to the flow of language which came from the lady of the house, who greeted us. Fortunately, the young man, her son, could speak some English. They gave us coffee and we explained that we were from the ship and had the rest of the day to explore.

As lunch time arrived, we said good-bye to our hospitable hosts and made our departure - but not before they had invited us to return in the evening for a little 'festa' which was to be held to celebrate the mother's birthday.

That afternoon, I hunted up 'many happy returns of the day' word by word, in the dictionary. Suitably prepared, we sallied forth to our first Brazilian party. There was a large room full of guests who all smiled their welcome, and we went up to our hostess and I greeted her with the phrase I had carefully rehearsed. To my surprise, everyone fell silent and looked at each other with embarrassment,

some smiling. The son turned away from me, shaking with laughter!
"José, what's the matter - what have I said wrong?" I asked him.
"Dona Jacquelina, you have just wished my mother many more
children and she already has fourteen!" Everyone was laughing by
now, and I begged José to ask his mother to forgive me. Happily, she
had a good sense of humour, and laughingly came and embraced
me. I didn't dare to try and say one more thing in Portuguese for
several days, but these dear, warm-hearted people had won my
affection already and I determined to master their language as fast
as possible so that I could communicate with them.

Our next and final stop was Recife, further down the coast.
Bert, or Eduardo as he was called in Brazil, who was the missionary
brother with whom we were to stay, had come from the interior to
meet us. We all stayed with a Swedish sister, who ran an orphanage.
Several days were spent in getting our luggage out of the Customs,
registering with the Police and buying food to take with us.

FIFTEEN

INITIATION AND TPREPIDATION

While in Recife, we attended the local church and marvelled at the crowd of about two thousand members, who sang and clapped to the music so enthusiastically. The Brazilian Pastor introduced us to his large flock, one by one - Alberto, Maria, Jacquelina and finally Gordon. When his name was announced, there was a ripple of laughter. They had adjusted our names to the Brazilian style but Gordon, or Gordo, meant 'fat one'. Gordon being robust in frame but certainly not fat, would obviously lose dignity if this name was used. Eduardo, the pastor and Sister Cisne held a conference over the matter. The problem was that Gordon didn't have a middle name. "Then we must give him a suitable one," said Eduardo. 'Steven' or 'Estevao' was finally chosen and Gordon was called this throughout our residence in the country.

The day for our departure finally came and we set off into the interior by car, very early. A truck was to follow later which was to carry our trunks along with its own load. The car stirred up the dust on the unpaved road. Patos, our destination was a small town set on a barren plateau, just below the Amazon. There was not much scenery to admire, only miles of flat, arid land dotted with large rocks, cacti and occasional scrub, but barely a tree to be seen. We stopped for a meal in Campina Grande - our first authentic Brazilian meal, and then set out on the last lap of our journey.

We arrived early in the evening to be greeted by Eduardo's wife, Dora, their little son, Graham, and Xandu, a half-Indian woman who lived with them. Hot, tired and covered in dust, we were glad to be shown the 'bathroom' which turned out to be a little hut at the bottom of the backyard where, one by one we carried our ration of hot water in a basin. Finally, we had supper, which consisted of bean soup, bread and butter, some cheese and coffee. Soon afterwards we went to our rooms and were shown how to lie in a hammock. In spite of the initial difficulties in sleeping in this way, none of us stayed awake for very long.

The next morning we were up early, eager to see around the town and to become initiated into our new life. After a breakfast of bread and butter, home-made marmalade and coffee, we had our devotions in Portuguese and English. We were given instructions regarding correct behaviour, dress and so forth and then we started out on our tour of the town. We acquainted ourselves with the few shops, Bank, Post Office and other amenities available and then returned in time for eleven o'clock lunch. Since it was very hot by then, we were glad to be able to enjoy the comparative coolness inside the house. Lunch consisted of rice with beans cooked with pieces of meat, pumpkin and okra, followed by juicy pineapples. Our menus throughout varied little, except for lettuce and tomatoes which were only available during several months of the year. The choice of fruit also depended on the season. Sweetcorn came on the market in June and then we had a feast! We could get different types of bananas at all times, including one which had to be cooked before eating. After lunch and washing-up we lay in our hammocks for about an hour or so, just running with perspiration. There were no fans or refrigerators, though rich people in the area did have them.

The rest of the time was spent in language study and doing other jobs before meeting together again for the evening meal called 'jantar'. After this we made ourselves ready for the meeting.

On our arrival in the small hall, we were presented to the local Christians, of whom there were about eighty - quite a good number for a church in the interior. The Roman Catholics had a strong hold on the whole of Northern Brazil.

We found that we knew the music of many of the hymns, as they had been translated from the English hymnals, which was a great help. It was interesting to see that all the men were on one side and all the women on the other. We had already realized that women were definitely second-class citizens! However, several of them were wearing very pretty, fashionable dresses, with high-heeled, dainty sandals. I thought ruefully of my Army boots. The poorer women, however, wore flat, simple leather sandals made for hard wear on the rough roads. We were later told that the girls put all their money on their backs, as it were, and that they were good dressmakers. It was certainly hard to believe that many of these prettily-dressed girls lived in dirt-floored mud huts!

Then came Sunday and we were again briefed by Eduardo. Contrary to our expectations, there was only Sunday School in the morning, which was for all ages, and this started at 9:30 am after we'd done our shopping. Shopping on Sunday? Our thoughts went back to England, where some folk would rather die, almost, than shop on Sunday! However, as Eduardo smilingly said, if we wanted to live in Brazil we must get used to the idea of buying the bulk of our food on Sunday mornings.

After breakfast, at about seven o'clock, a young boy came to the house with a large basket on his head, and we all set off for the market. This was a fascinating experience once we had overcome the guilty feelings of breaking the Sabbath! People came in from miles around to sell their beans, rice, chickens, fruit and other produce. Little boys with large baskets on their heads ran around, seeking patrons to hire them for a few cruzeiros. Still younger ones had trays of lollipops to sell. The first item was fresh meat. The swarms of flies buzzing round this stall put us off and we turned away, leaving Eduardo to do the bargaining for our week's supply. Our basket filled up gradually but it was a slow business as our brother haggled over every item. Gordon watched this process with special interest - it was just in his line! I was thankful that the husbands did the shopping for many of the families - I knew I wouldn't be very successful in bargaining!

At last it was finished and we went home, just in time to catch the water-man making his rounds. He rode from house to house on his patient mule, with kerosene tins filled with water hanging from panniers on each side. Dora bought two tins and the man poured the water into large clay pots, through squares of white muslin. By the time he had finished, the cloth was no longer white! I thought of the Scripture, "and if you shall drink of any deadly thing it shall not hurt you." I could see that we'd often need to remind ourselves of that! Of course, we had to boil the water we used for drinking and then pour it into a separate jug. As there was no 'fridge to cool it in, it would have to stand for hours before it could be used to quench our frequent thirst.

By this time Xandu had cut off a piece from the goat's meat for dinner and had salted the rest, hanging it in the corner of the kitchen to dry. For the rest of the week she would cut off a piece each day, soak it for a couple of hours in water and then cook it with the beans for about three hours. The cooking was done over a fire of dried wood called 'lenha' or charcoal which was more expensive. One had to fan the fire frequently, which was hot work.

SIXTEEN

"NEW GROUND"

We were all to stay with Dora and Eduardo until we could speak enough of the language to get around on our own. We had so much to learn, besides the language. Our laundry had to go out in a big bundle every few days to a washerwoman who would bring it back afterwards, washed and ironed. We went along to see the 'laundry'. The women were crouched by the edge of the stream, which had been a wide river a few months previously. The drought then prevailing had reduced it to a slow-running dribble of water. After soap had been rubbed on, the garments were pounded with a small rock. I shuddered, wondering how long our cotton clothes would stand up to this treatment! Dirty patches that didn't respond to this process were well soaped again and laid out to dry in the sun, before being re-washed. Once the articles were clean, they were spread out over rocks and prickly bushes to dry. Sometimes we found tiny holes in our clothes - a souvenir from the prickly bushes!

After three months, confident that we had learned to deal with nearly every aspect of life in this land, we started looking for a suitable home for ourselves at an affordable price. Gordon and I were the first to move out, and bought a second-hand kitchen table and four chairs, large water pots and other basics for our home. Mary and Albert had brought out a couple of deck chairs which were ideal for relaxing in but we hadn't thought of that, so Gordon decided he would make his own armchair.

After the various parts had been cut out (we had brought a do-it-yourself manual with us) Gordon fitted them together, in preparation for finally sticking and nailing the chair. Just as he had done this, a visitor called - no less a person than a Portuguese teacher who taught English at the local High School. We invited him in and put out a chair for him to sit on but he ignored it and before we could say a word, he had sat on the unfinished chair, which promptly collapsed under him. Unfortunately, the young man did not have a sense of humour and didn't think the incident was funny, even though we explained what we had been doing and apologized. After a few minutes of conversation he took his leave in a decidedly cool manner, never to visit us again. Gordon then finished the chair, having made a very good job of it.

By this time I was several months pregnant with our first child. Fortunately, I'd brought a book with me on preparing for natural childbirth as the baby would be born at home, with only the aid of a Brazilian midwife. Happily, there was a Christian one in town, called Maria da Conceicao.

Our own Mary found this name business rather disconcerting. If you called out "Maria" in a loud enough voice, half the street would erupt with answering women! The same way, if you called out "Jose", half the male inhabitants would respond. The Brazilians had their own way of resolving the matter, with regard to the women, anyway. There were about forty varieties - Maria da Conceicao, Maria da Fatima, Maria da Lua and so on, corresponding to the names given to the Virgin Mary. The girls honoured with these names would there-fore answer to 'Conceicao', 'Lua' and suchlike.

Our own Mary had no such attachment to her name which rather confused the Brazilians. "You're Maria what?" they would ask, and as no surnames were ever used in addressing people, she would have to reply, "Just Maria." Fortunately, the surnames were long appendages used only for registering births, school attendance, weddings and deaths. Our poor English names sounded so inferior to the high-sounding Brazilian names.

SEVENTEEN

VISITATION WORK-THE HARD WAY

Those were busy days. It took us almost all our time just to live. After we had been in our little home for about three months, Eduardo thought it was time to take Gordon and Albert on a visit to some of the preaching outposts, several hours' journey away. Mary was still with Dora but I would be left on my own. I packed Gordon's clothes and saw him off very early one morning with Eduardo and Albert.

The first stage of their journey involved getting a ride on the back of a cotton-truck (for which they had to pay!) and travelling for some three hours on top of cotton bales with no protection from the sun. At the end of this leg of their journey, they picked up mules from a farm belonging to one of the Christians, and travelled for many hours, visiting one lonely farm or village after another. Riding in the intense heat, with irregular, sparse meals, told on Albert and Gordon - Albert got dysentery. Eduardo, although quite a bit older than the other two, was acclimatized. In spite of the hardships involved, the men loved the work. They received such warm hospitality and appreciation from the people. On arrival at a homestead, Eduardo would clap his hands and usually one of the men would come out. If it was the house of a Christian, they would be welcomed into the house, but where non-Christians lived Eduardo would be asked a barrage of questions - were the men married - did they have families, etc.? When satisfactorily answered they would be allowed to dismount and enter the house, where they would be offered water and coffee. Meanwhile the women would all retire into the back of the house.

At a Christian home, the welcome was always warm and

demonstrative. Our men soon became accustomed to being embraced by the Brazilian men - so different from the simple handshake which they were used to in England. No sooner had they dismounted than the family would gather round and eagerly ask for news of the church and family. A young man would be sent to the nearest Christian neighbours and others in the vicinity to inform them of the arrival of the missionaries. While syrupy coffee was served, more often than not someone went out to kill an unfortunate chicken or goat. Albert and Gordon were carefully examined and, when the family realized that they didn't understand much Brazilian, comments were made about their appearance! However, it was all done with affection and good humour.

After a while, they would be given hammocks and allowed to rest until the meal was ready. Once the men were all seated, the women folk would wait on them, continually filling their plates as they ate, eating themselves only after the men had finished. Once the meal was over, the neighbours would begin to arrive and Albert would produce his concertina. Wooden benches were brought out and people would often be packed in like sardines. In that sparsely populated area, it was difficult to understand where they had all come from! Then the meeting would start. What hearty singing - no matter if it was often out of tune! The Brazilians are no nightingales at the best of times, but what they lacked in quality they certainly made up for in volume.

Eduardo interpreted for Gordon and Albert as they testified and then he preached. The meeting would last for two or three hours - after all, the English brothers wouldn't be around again for several weeks and so they were determined to make the most of it!

Reluctantly, they would allow Eduardo to close the meeting, and the visitors would leave for their homes. Usually several among them would be rejoicing in their new found salvation. Then our men would sink into their hammocks, hung up in the living room, trying to ignore the livestock that would often be sharing their bedroom. One night, Gordon had to get out of his hammock to go outside. As he lowered himself on to the ground, there was an ear-splitting squeal - he had disturbed the slumbers of a pig, who disliked being used as a stepping-stool!

The following morning, after coffee and bananas, (there was no bread), the three men would start off again, travelling for two to three hours on their mules across the dry, dusty plateau. Miles away in the background, they would see the Araripe mountains. On their arrival at the next homestead on their schedule, the same procedure as before would be followed. After about two weeks of this, the three men returned home. Worn out and travel-sore, they would barely be able to sit down! How happy they were to relate their experiences to us, and share their joy in reporting the number of souls added to the Church! Gordon suffered feelings of tremendous frustration at not being able to preach the Gospel in Brazilian. He so longed to be able to communicate the Good News to the people, so once again he got down to the grim process of studying the language.

EIGHTEEN

HOW TO MAKE FRIENDS

Soon there came a point when Gordon was sufficiently fluent to start a dental clinic for the poor in Patos. Although one already existed, unless the patient had the money to pay for the injection, their teeth would be extracted without! Needless to say, as Gordon always gave injections even when they couldn't pay, his clientele grew rapidly! The small sums paid by those who could afford it, just about covered our expenses. This dentistry work, done in our backyard, took all our mornings and as Gordon's reputation for gentleness and efficiency grew, it became difficult to fit all the patients into the time we had available. Syphilis was rampant in the blood stream of many so the injections wouldn't always take, and unfortunately not all the operations were painless. I think we suffered as much as the patients when we saw that the injections were not taking effect! The patients always insisted that Gordon proceed with the extraction, however. They were courageous people!

We had gradually become accustomed to our new life. To fit all of our household chores into our busy schedule, we had to rise very early in the morning. Before preparing breakfast, I had to cut off a piece of meat from the salted lump, and soak it until it was time to cook the beans. The first time I had salted the meat in my own home, I had hung it to dry just outside the back door. After a few minutes Gordon gave a shout and I rushed out just in time to see a big vulture flying off with our week's precious supply of meat.

The heat and the flies were our worst trials. The heat, which reached 120°F during several months of the year, was almost unbearable by mid-day. If we put a bare foot on to the cement outside the door, it would burn. One could fry an egg on the pavement at mid-day! Now we knew why Patos was called the Inferno of the North!

As for the flies, they were everywhere. We didn't have the money to put screens in the windows and doors. Meal times were the worst. One day, in desperation, I suggested that we hang a mosquito net up in the living room and eat our meal under it, so we could eat in peace. We tried this, but before dinner was over, it seemed as if all the flies had come in to join us! Finally, we crawled out from under the net, took it outside and emptied it into the yard.

By now Gordon's reputation as a good dentist had drawn a number of patients from among the comfortably-off citizens, which upset the dentists in town. They sent a delegation to the Mayor, who then told Gordon he could no longer practice in town but only in the outskirts from then on.

For some time I had been suffering from toothache and Gordon said it was due to a bad molar. As I felt I could trust Gordon to do a good job, he prepared to extract the tooth. We had to close all the windows and doors, so that nobody could see us - we didn't want to risk Gordon being seen, in case somebody had reported it to the authorities. They might think Gordon was ignoring the ban on doing dentistry in town. I have never had a better piece of work done on my teeth!

In the afternoons, after our siesta we would sometimes receive visitors. One young man called Eddie Polo, would come to our house frequently to speak English with us. He was a student and the son of an Army Major. He told us about the death of his father, who had been murdered two years previously as the result of a family feud. Such feuds are not uncommon in the North, and it appeared that the matter started a generation back. The Major had been killed for something for which he had not been responsible. Family pride was at stake and, as was the custom, the eldest son of the house was duty-bound to take revenge. Eddie lived for the day he would avenge the death of his father.

In the North, if a man was not caught within three days of

committing a murder, he was not charged with the crime. It was a comparatively easy matter to hide from the police in that vast area. Killings were so frequent that the police did not exert themselves unduly in hunting out the murderers. Every man and some women, too, were armed to the teeth with knives in their belts, up their sleeves or hidden in some other place. Those who could afford to do so carried a pistol. In that hot climate tempers would fray easily over an argument and rage would quickly dominate a man. Hardly knowing what they were doing, a man would reach for his knife or gun and the quickest on the draw would be the victor. When it happened outside the town, a cross would be set up on the site of the killing. We saw many such crosses as we travelled around.

I remember visiting the wife of a police sergeant one day. While I was there, a sinister looking man called on some errand or other. I noticed how my hostess and her daughter 'froze' when he came in, and when he had gone, and they relaxed, they told me that he was a notorious killer who managed continually to evade the law! He had shaken hands with me and now I instinctively wiped my hands on my dress with a shudder!

We had many conversations with Eddie and prayed for him continually. Dominated by the knowledge that one day he would have to kill, he adamantly refused to open his heart to the Lord. He had no brother to whom he could delegate the grisly task and he could not contemplate failing to fulfill what he regarded as his duty. His family were Catholics but somehow the Scripture, "Vengeance is mine, saith the Lord," was either never taught or else it was ignored by the people. Eddie hated his father's killer with a cold, implacable hatred. After a time his visits saddened us, as we realized that this passion blinded him completely to the Gospel. When we left the district, we could only commit him to the Lord, and trust in Him to water the seed we had planted. We never heard of Eddie again.

NINETEEN

Seeing these results of spiritual death among the people strengthened our determination and desire to minister the precious Gospel to them at whatever cost. The Lord saw this desire and commitment and led us into strange and difficult paths in order to manifest his love for these ignorant and wayward people. One incident in particular, which added fuel to the fire in our hearts occurred at this time.

We heard a commotion up the street where we lived. Gordon hurried out to see what was happening and saw a small crowd gathered outside a house. When he got there, he found that the occupier, a young woman, was dying. She was in a room that opened on to the street and the shutters were open. The screams of this poor soul had attracted a crowd of men - she was a prostitute. One man called out, "Send for the priest, Maria," then another shouted, "Pray to Our Lady."

Gordon pushed through the crowd until he was near the window. He saw her, stretching herself up against the wall, clawing at it as she cried out for help. She sank to the floor and then tried to lift herself up again, digging her nails into the plaster. Oblivious to the calls of the men, she screamed out hoarsely, "I'm lost, I'm lost!"

Gordon, moved to the depths of his being, called out the Word of the Lord to her - "Everyone who calls on the Name of the Lord shall be saved." Acts 2:21.

She turned her face toward him. "It's too late," she moaned, "too late!" Gordon then gave her more of the Word, telling her to call on Jesus and He would save her. He told her of the thief who was crucified at the side of Jesus, and how Jesus had told him that he would be in paradise with him that very day. Within a few minutes she had sunk, for the last time, dying to the floor. The men around her were quiet. As Gordon walked home he wondered whether or not the Words that he had quoted to her had sunk into that poor, anguished heart and enabled her to lay hold of Jesus in her extremity.

After hearing this, I felt spurred on to apply myself still harder to studying the language. No feeling attacks a missionary so strongly as the frustration at not being able to communicate, when people around are living and dying in such darkness and hopelessness. These people, as courageous and strong as they were in facing the rigors and sufferings of their daily lives, "through fear of death were all their lifetime subject to bondage," as the Bible so aptly puts it - Hebrews 2:15. Fear of dying at the hand of another often moved them to make the first knife-thrust. Fear of purgatory made them take their hard-earned money to pay for Masses to be said on behalf of their dead loved ones: money often needed to buy food for the living. Fear, fear, fear - it dominated their lives. It crushed them with burdens they had little strength to bear. "Oh Lord, help me to prepare myself to take Your wonderful News to these dear people!" was my continual prayer.

The love in our hearts overcame all the small feelings of revulsion that we sometimes felt at their crude habits. We disciplined ourselves not to show any sign of shrinking from any native custom. The people were quick to sense any withdrawal in a foreigner and this could ruin promising relationships. The greatest test as to how well I had learned to relate to Brazilian peasants came when we had only been in the country about five months.

The Annual Conference was due to be held at a farm right out in the wild. Several members of the local church were going to accompany us missionaries and expectations ran high.

TWENTY

A COUNTRY CONFERENCE

The great day came and we all boarded the two trucks that were to take us the greater part of the journey. As foreign women, we were privileged to sit in front with the drivers. After about three hours, we were dropped off at a turning, from where we had to make the rest of the journey by mule or by foot. Again, being foreigners, we women were given mules. The rest of the party trudged along happily on foot, some removing their precious shoes to do so. We had learned that the Christians would walk miles to attend a meeting, carrying their shoes until they came to the town or meeting. Then they would wipe their feet and put on their shoes.

After a pleasant ride, we arrived at the farm, where we were offered water and coffee to drink. The place hummed with activity and we could hear the raucous squawks of the chickens as they met their final fate. All was hustle and bustle in the kitchen, where the women were preparing the food. Dora warned us not to go in the kitchen while they were cooking - she said we would lose our appetites if we did so! Being really hungry, we agreed to do as she advised. We were only too glad to relax in the hammocks that had been put up for us under the awning outside the farmhouse. When we asked where the toilets were, Dora chuckled and told us that they didn't bother to put up notices to distinguish which bushes were for women and which for men. It was just accepted that women went one side and men the other! Fortunately, forewarned, we had brought our own toilet paper with us.

Before jantar was served, we were asked if we would like to wash. The main heat of the day was over and we felt sweaty and sticky, so we welcomed the idea with alacrity. Owing to a shortage of basins, we had to wash one at a time. Dora, armed with her soap and towel, followed our hostess to a convenient clump of bushes and was left there. When she emerged, Mary and I followed suit, and then we all joined the men who had also had their wash. Jantar was then served.

Again, we English women were allowed to eat with the men at the huge trestle tables, which were piled high with dishes of rather 'gooey' rice, huge platters of chicken and dishes of ground mandioca root - rather like fine white sawdust to look at and taste! However, the Brazilians heaped spoonfuls of it on to their beans and rice, mixed it up, made it into small balls with their fingers and threw them into their mouths. Our men tried to copy them - without much success - accompanied by roars of laughter, so we decided to eat ours with the spoons so thoughtfully provided. It all tasted very good, and as fast as we ate the women behind us would fill our plates again until we begged them to stop! Then we walked around a bit while the women ate, as it was now cooler.

We walked down to the pond, where the animals were having a drink, their hooves in the water. Clothes were drying on bushes round about. Then the women came down with small water pots and filled them with water from the pond. We followed them back to the house, and watched while they emptied them into large jars, passing the water through muslin squares as we did. I watched with fascination the tiny bugs and particles of pond life left in the muslin. Never again, would I ask for a glass of water in a farmhouse! Fortunately, our contemplation was interrupted by the announcement that the meeting would start in a few minutes.

Believers were coming in from all directions and the air rang with "A paz do Senhor," - "the peace of God be with you". It was the customary greeting of one believer to another. We went to collect our Bibles and hymn-books. I looked at Mary, thinking she looked rather pale. Poor girl, it was worse for her; being a nurse, she knew much more than we did about the embryonic diseases that the water could contain!

The meeting started. Night had fallen and the little lamps, tin pots of kerosene with wicks stuck in, were giving forth a smoky light and smell. The storm lamp we had brought with us brightened up the house. Albert brought his concertina out and we were off!

Such singing and praying, followed by messages given by our husbands, then more singing and praying! Finally the meeting ended and we got up stiffly from the backless benches on which we had been sitting. When we had said our goodbyes to the visiting brethren, we retired to our hammocks in the living-room which we shared with several chickens. At least there were no pigs - they were put in with the menfolk. Tired but happy I fell off to sleep!

Dawn came and the household stirred. We rolled up our hammocks and went out into the cool air. Later coffee was served with bananas - no bread out there! The chores done and a young goat having been slaughtered for the meal, we all prepared for the morning meeting. Visitors started arriving and benches were set out. Again we had rousing singing and the preaching was listened to with avid interest. Lunch time came, after which everyone rested in the heat of the afternoon. We had brought fans with us, and used them to ward off the flies. The time came to prepare for jantar, to be followed by the evening meeting.

Without thinking, I wandered into the kitchen. The house had a dirt floor and no ceiling. Thick rafters stretched across while baked tiles roofed the low building. The fireplace was in the middle of the kitchen, on the floor, and big pots sat on top of the burning wood. As I looked, the rice overflowed and some spilled onto the floor. It was quickly scooped up again and put back into the pot. Something fell from the rafters into the pot of beans, and it got stirred in as the cook was watching the rice and didn't notice. I went out to join the others but said nothing to them about what I'd seen! I ate very carefully that evening and with not quite such a good appetite as usual. I saw Gordon surreptitiously slide a stewed cockroach off his dish and under the edge. He did not wish to upset our kind hosts who had done their best for us. How they loved us, these dear people!

The Conference over, we wended our way back home. It had been a happy time and none of us suffered any ill consequences. God is faithful to His Word!

TWENTY-ONE

*"IN THE DAYS OF FAMINE, THEY SHALL
BE SATISFIED" PSALM 37:19*

The weeks passed by and still no rain. The situation was very serious - two and a half years without rain! The people became desperate. The cattle that remained were just thin skeletons and the crops failed. Lorry loads of men took off for the South, where they hoped to find work. Some died on the way and there was usually no work for those who got to Sao Paulo, an industrialized city. Those who remained joined the queues outside the monasteries, to which the government sent some supplies for the poor. We discovered that some of the rich people sent their servants to receive some of the food! In some cases, fathers would kill their wives and children, then themselves, because they couldn't bear to see their families starve to death. Every day, children would come to our door, often with a baby brother or sister on their backs, begging for food. It broke our hearts to see how little we had to give them. Our friends in England couldn't help - the British government had restricted money being sent out to the country to a very small pittance, barely enough for us to live on. One day, a group of peasants raided the market, taking away sacks of beans and rice. The food that was available had risen in price - beyond their pitiful means. Men had to dig holes in the river-beds to find water.

This area had once been very productive, but they had cut all the trees down. Long droughts were now common occurrence. No reservoirs had been built or other provision made for these periods. The Northeast was forgotten by the rest of the country.

None of our Christians had to leave their farms, however. The testimony of one and all was that the Lord had provided for them and they always had something to eat.

In one case, a Christian farmer took Gordon to see his sugar cane, which was flourishing, and told him an interesting story: His neighbour was involved in voodoo and hated him. One day, the neighbour cursed the sugar cane within the hearing of our brother who promptly threw the curse back on to his neighbour's cane. As a result, the neighbour's cane became withered and burnt up, while that of the believer flourished. From then on the neighbour showed the Christian great respect!

One morning we found that we had run out of food. We drank our last drop of coffee and ate our last piece of bread, then Gordon set off for the Bank. Our remittance was overdue and we hoped that it had now arrived. Gordon returned looking rather glum - the money hadn't arrived. I was now six months pregnant and shouldn't fast, as we had done on other 'sticky' occasions. We sought the Lord and were reminded of a verse; Philippians 4:19 - "My God shall supply all your needs according to His riches in glory in Christ Jesus." We reminded Him of His Word and decided that we would not make our needs known to anyone but the Lord. Then we just carried on with our usual occupations.

Later that morning, a chicken flew into our yard. There were always a few picking around in the wasteland outside, so Gordon threw the bird out. A few minutes later the chicken came in again. This was too much of a temptation for Gordon who promptly shut it in the hut that was our bathroom.

An hour passed - "Oh, that poor bird!" said Gordon, "I must let it out - it certainly won't come in here tempting me again!" He opened the door and as the bird flew out over the wall, Gordon noticed something white on the floor in the corner - an egg! How we laughed! "This is better than Elijah's ravens," Gordon chuckled. I had the egg and although he had to fast, he didn't mind. The Lord had heard our cry and we knew he would continue to undertake for us.

The following morning, Gordon again went to the Bank but the money still hadn't come in. However, we committed our situation to the Lord with renewed faith and expectancy. How would He supply our need today? We were soon to find out. I asked the Lord to send enough for Gordon this time!

At 11:30 a.m., our usual lunch-time, there was a knock at the door. As I opened it I saw a pretty young woman, whom I didn't know, holding a large tray of food. She handed it to me without a word and I took it automatically, but before I could recover my powers of speech she had fled. As Gordon came up I handed him the heavy tray and sat down. We looked at the contents - a cooked chicken, rice, bread and fruit. We just lifted up our hands and worshipped our heavenly Father. What provision!

That food lasted us for three days, after which our money arrived. We didn't learn who our benefactor was for three weeks, when we discovered that she attended a tiny Baptist church in town. She had felt impressed to send us that food, and later, out of curiosity to know why she had felt like that, she came to our church to find out. With Eduardo's help all this was interpreted to us and we rejoiced together over our wonderful Lord, who will lead us in such wonderful ways when we are sensitive to His directions!

Our sister had been especially shy about revealing her identity because the Brazilians couldn't imagine us being in need. They thought that all foreigners were well off and that it was sheer eccentricity on our part that made us live like the poor! From then on, the people looked at us as being like themselves, and felt more at home with us.

A few days later, Gordon had to go to the coast, to meet a brother missionary who was returning from furlough. Remembering the good things we had enjoyed on our voyage, Gordon said that he would endeavour to make friends with the Chief Steward on our friend's boat, and try to get some items of food that were unattainable in Brazil. After three days he returned with a large brown paper parcel. I had visions of good English chocolate, jams and suchlike. I thought Gordon looked a bit sheepish, hopwever, as he watched me undo the parcel. The reason became apparent as I was faced with packets of tea - nothing but tea! Knowing Gordon's love for the beverage, I couldn't help laughing and forgave him for forgetting the other items I had requested.

One day a man came along with a young chicken. He offered it to Gordon quite cheaply, telling him that when it was older it would lay good eggs. Gordon, always on the lookout for a bargain, haggled a little and paid for the fowl. He made a box for it and gave it the best corn. The bird grew but still no eggs - we couldn't understand it. Then a brother from the country came in one day and Gordon showed him the bird, explaining that it didn't lay any eggs, and asked him for advice. He roared with laughter. "That bird will never lay eggs...it's a cock-bird!" The story went around the preaching circuit and for a long time the believers used to slyly ask him if he was still hoping to get eggs from his cock! From that day, the bird's days were numbered, and Gordon enjoyed the meal made from it more than any other!

TWENTY-TWO

A PREDICTION COMES TO PASS

Sure enough it was a year since the staff of the Maternity Hospital in Portadown had predicted that I would have a baby within a year! I could imagine their chuckles when they heard of the event.

We acquired a bed, with a firm grass mattress, and the time grew near for the birth of the baby. I had made some clothes for it and all was ready. One evening I sent Gordon for Conçeiçáo. It was January - one of the hottest months of the year, but I had to close the wooden shutters across the glass-less windows because some of the neighbours were gathering outside to see how the foreigner behaved while in labour! The room was stifling, as the only air there was came in through the tiles on the roof, especially the ones the vultures had broken!

Wendy really took her time and twenty-one hours passed before she finally made her entrance into the world, helped by Gordon who had come in to pray with us. Conçeiçáo had wanted to send for a doctor but being afraid that he would use forceps I refused. Wendy weighed eight pounds seven ounces and was a beautiful baby.

Having only Gordon to care for me, who was a firm believer in oatmeal porridge to stimulate my milk, I lived on the stuff for nearly three days until I was well enough to get up and cook our meals. Conçeiçáo came in to help with the baby for the first few days.

Midwifery is a lucrative profession in Brazil, where large families - up to fourteen or more - are commonplace. Conçeiçáo enjoyed considerable prestige in town and now would be able to say she had delivered an English baby and ask even more money from her customers! Wendy thrived and this little blue-eyed blonde was the delight of our home. We were a happy little family.

The men made another trip further into the interior but this time they split up. Gordon was accompanied by the son of one of the bandits who had been recently converted. When we first arrived in Brazil, there were still a number of small bandit communities scattered over the plateau. Lampeáo, their famed leader, had been caught, along with some of the others, and their heads were now preserved in alcohol in Fortaleza, the state capital of the coast. The rest had divided up, evading the soldiers, and were allowed to live undisturbed in their villages. The police warned our men not to visit them but of course they did, taking with them as their only armament the Sword of the Spirit, the Bible. The Lord saved several of them and their families, and Gordon later returned with his dental equipment to extract some of their teeth.

One ex-bandit, Antonio da Onça he was called, because he was supposed to have killed a bear, had a very bad tooth. He asked Gordon to take it out, which he prepared to do. Antonio had had a very bad reputation as a killer, and had not known the Lord very long. The injection did not take, owing to syphilis in his blood, but Antonio told Gordon to go ahead anyway, as he didn't think it could hurt anymore than it did already! He still wore one knife and Gordon admitted afterwards that he had kept one eye on his work and one on the knife!

When the tooth finally came out, Gordon showed it to Antonio who growled, saying that if it had been a year ago, he would have had his knife in Gordon! These occupational hazards didn't worry Gordon unduly, and he continued to help these outcasts of society.

Later when Gordon was sharing experiences with another missionary, down South, the American told him that when he was once in the North, he had been kidnapped by Lampeáo himself. The bandit had sent one of his men to Virgil's partner, demanding money or he'd kill Virgil. Of course, the partner had very little money but gave it to the bandit. Lampeáo was furious, saying that he wasn't asking for alms and would kill Virgil! Our brother asked him if he may say a few words to him and his men first, which Lampeáo allowed, and Virgil gave them the Gospel. Lampeáo then told one of his men to take Virgil back to the road near his home and they blindfolded him until they were well away from the bandits' camp and then released him.

To return to the account of Gordon's journey with the bandit's son, Blackie. He was tall and lanky, with a mixture of both Indian and Portuguese blood, and had all the cunning that was so typical for the blend. They travelled by mule for a couple of days, visiting small congregations. At night they would share a room in a typical country 'pensao' or boarding-house. The rooms were just cubicles divided by low partitions with doors that couldn't be locked.

One morning, Gordon couldn't find his socks, which he had hung on the end of his hammock. "They must have been stolen while we were sleeping," he commented to Blackie. "Fancy someone stealing a missionary's socks - he is 'sem vergonha' - without shame!" said Blackie.

Gordon put on another pair and then they mounted their mules and were off. They travelled quietly for a while then, looking down, Gordon happened to notice of Blackies feet, almost touching the ground. Beneath the edge of his trousers Gordon could see a small area of sock - his sock! Blackie was wearing his socks! Gordon stifled an involuntary exclamation - to even hint that a man was a thief could provoke a knife thrust, and he wasn't too sure of the extent of Blackie's spiritual commitment. He decided to say nothing - after all he thought, chuckling to himself, the early church had all things in common. Thank God for a sense of humour!

TWENTY-THREE

"A KERNAL OF WHEAT FALLS TO THE GROUND AND DIES"
JOHN 12:24

A few days later, they were travelling through wild country, on a narrow track through the bush, when Gordon suddenly became aware that Blackie was no longer behind him. He was alone, miles from any village, and without his guide he had no idea how to reach his destination. He sent up an S.O.S. to the Lord and, as he quieted his spirit he received the answer, Trust in the mule.' Now if there was one animal Gordon never trusted, it was the mule! "Did you say, 'trust in the mule' Lord?" He wondered if he was hearing right. "Trust in the mule," came the answer again, and so he slackened his hold on the reins. For the next few hours he gave the mule her head, becoming more and more anxious as the day wore on. However, just as he was beginning to give up hope of finding the farm, they arrived! There was no sign of Blackie, who evidently had an assignment of his own. The family was very glad to see Gordon and listened with interest when he told them what had happened. Then they laughed and told him that a mule, when left to its own devices, will always make for home, and that this particular mule had actually come from their farm!

Gordon returned from his trip very satisfied. In spite of his still limited knowledge of the language, eight people had accepted Jesus as their Saviour. Gordon realized more and more, that it was a case of giving the people the Word of God, with as few of his own words as possible! The Word did its own work in the hearts of the hearers!

We had been told about the terrible epidemics of gastroenteritis that hit the Northeastern area practically every year. At that time, the infant mortality rate of babies under two years of age was 95%. A new drug was coming out to combat this but hadn't reached this backward area yet. Eduardo and Dora had lost a little girl to this plague. The awful swarms of flies, poor and often non-existent sanitation, great heat and lack of medical care all contributed to this terrible scourge. It was difficult to find a family that had not lost at least one baby through it. We did all we could to protect Wendy but she caught it. However, within a few days the Lord healed her. She was now a year old.

Mary and Albert were the first to leave Patos for another town, some four hours away, that had never had the Gospel. About three months later Eduardo and Gordon set out on a journey to another area that was also without the Gospel that would take them a day to reach. Before they left, however, Gordon suggested that Wendy and I go to stay with Mary and Albert while he was away. Wendy hadn't been very well and it was a little cooler in their town than in Patos. He put the two of us into a jeep that was going that way and we said goodbye. After bumping for hours along bad roads we arrived at our destination.

I found our colleagues rather depressed. No one ever came to their meetings - the people were quite polite but completely indifferent to their efforts to interest them in the Gospel. They had recently had some political elections and quite a lot of shooting had taken place so Mary's nursing skills had come in very useful and the people were grateful. Albert and Mary were beginning to wonder if they had come to the right place. I tried to encourage them and we prayed together about the situation, but I wasn't too happy myself. Wendy's health was not improving and there were signs that she had gastroenteritis again. I sought the Lord but could not find assurance that He would heal her.

As Mary and I did some visiting we heard of other cases of this plague in the town. Wendy's sickness drew the attention of some of the women to us - we had something in common as we endeavoured to save the lives of our precious babies. There was no doctor and none could be called over from another town. The bridge across the river had collapsed due to the rains which had finally come, cutting us from the rest of the world.

I remembered having read the story of the death of a missionary's baby in the Congo, a few weeks previously, and of how it had hit me. I had thought, suppose the Lord should take my Wendy, but quickly put the idea out of my mind. I couldn't help wondering, however, if the Lord had been speaking to me, in preparation for what lay ahead. Now I knew.

Sitting there, watching our beautiful golden-haired darling grow weaker and weaker, just tore at my heart. Mary suggested I go for a walk while she took over the caring for Wendy. Every three hours or so I would do this. I felt led to visit other homes where the dreaded disease had struck, and as I saw the hopeless looks on the faces of the poor mothers, I began to realize the difference between us. As they sat there, burning candles around the hammocks of their dying babies, they had nothing to look forward to. Their babies had been 'baptized' by the priest and on that account they believed they would go to heaven, but what about them - would they ever get there and see their little ones again? How long would they have to spend in purgatory before they would be allowed in heaven? They were poor and couldn't afford many masses for all the members of their families who died. Their grief was dreadful to see. I knew that I would be reunited with Wendy again as soon as I died and this expectation took the sting out of death for me.

Filled with questions, such as why the Lord should take her, I knew deep down, there is a reason for everything that happens in the lives of Christians, even if we can't see it at the time.

Dear Lord, we have left everything to serve you in this country!" I cried. "Why are you taking Wendy from us?" Amidst all of the agony of seeing her dying, peace came into my heart, as I relinquished our little sweetheart into the arms of our loving Savior. I knew I must not yet give in to grief - the women of the town were watching me, to see how I took the death of my child. One had come to see us as Wendy lay dying.

When the news got around that she had passed away, the women started coming. Albert had stayed up late to make her little coffin and now she lay, like a little doll, by my side. The women filed by us, looking at me pityingly but the Lord gave me such grace that I was able to smile at the women and thank them for coming. As they left the house we could hear some of their remarks. "She is so quiet." "She has peace on her face." One woman said to us, "I have lost two babies like this," and I remarked quietly, "I haven't lost Wendy - I will be reunited with her in heaven, one day." I knew that this remark would be passed round the town.

We had sent a telegram to Gordon, hoping it would reach him. It eventually got to him but too late for him to return in time for Wendy's funeral. He arrived two days afterwards, as our bridge wasn't the only one that was down. Meanwhile, the Lord had ministered to him. Just before receiving the telegram, he had gone to a meeting and a sister in the Lord had given him a message in tongues which someone else interpreted. The Lord said that all that was happening was in His plan and not to doubt or grieve. Gordon knew instinctively that this word was for him.

I had asked Albert to preach the Gospel at Wendy's funeral. Brazilian women don't attend this last ceremony - a merciful custom, I think. When Albert and Mary came home afterwards, they were rejoicing. About two hundred people had come to the funeral! Albert had announced his meetings and afterwards, that night, several people attended and a few accepted Jesus as their Saviour. That was the beginning of the work in that town. Wendy's passing had made a bridge between the people and us. "Except a kernel of wheat falls into the ground and dies, it remains only a single seed; but if it dies it produces many seeds" - John 12:24. Out of the death of our little seed sprang much fruit!

When Gordon arrived, we decided there was no longer any reason to prevent us from moving into the town where we were to begin our ministry. Our little home in Patos held too many memories for me and I would be glad to leave it. We returned there to pack, leaving behind a happy couple who were expecting their first baby and who were experiencing the joy of seeing souls being born into the Kingdom of God.

TWENTY-FOUR

A GOOD FRIDAY TO BE REMEMBERED

It was a simple matter moving to Missao Velha. We had so few belongings, which went on by truck while we travelled by car and train. My heart was heavy as I thought of leaving little fifteen-months old Wendy, buried so far away from us. Yet I knew the real Wendy was not there - she was in heaven with Jesus. How I wished I could go there too! I knew, however, that we had only just started our work for the Lord. There was so much to do and it would be years, God willing, before I would be able to join Wendy and other loved ones up there. "Oh Lord, give me strength!" I cried. I felt so weak - the months of heat, inadequate food and breast-feeding Wendy, had taken their toll. I had ulcers all over my legs and feet which refused to heal. Exhausted both physically and emotionally I didn't feel able to face starting the work. There was just Gordon and I amongst thousands of people, many of whom would be hostile. It was going to be hard.

I didn't let Gordon see my tears. He was enthusiastic and welcomed the challenge. "We must go very quietly," he said, "making friends and seeing the lie of the land. There is a young and zealous priest in charge here and I know he won't take kindly to our presence!" There was also a seminary for training young priests right across the road from us!

We moved into the little house that Gordon had managed to rent, and bought a few necessities. In spite of my hurts, I began to take interest in the place. Here we were, really on our own. Our nearest missionary neighbours were about three or four hours drive from us - a group of American Baptist missionaries. How would we be received?

Perhaps it was a good thing that we were ignorant of what was happening behind the scenes. The peaceful atmosphere of the place was deceptive. A small party of German priests had been through the area, just before we had arrived, and had told the leading Catholics that the Protestants were gradually penetrating further and further into the Northeast. "You must keep them out at all costs." they said. Did they know the violent reactions their words would provoke...did they care if they led to the death of a young British couple?

It was Easter and we had been in the town ten days. Gordon had spent the time going round and getting to know people. I had left the house only once, because of the ulcers on my feet, but on this occasion as I walked slowly down the street, a lady had stopped to speak to me. She was a very pleasant, educated person, and we had a nice chat. As we parted, she said we must meet again soon for another talk. As I returned home, I thought with pleasure of seeing her again.

We spent the Good Friday at home, while the town carried out its usual Easter ritual. As we thought it better to keep away from their religious activities, we didn't see the large bonfire in the square, around which people were gathered. Neither did we see the two effigies burning on top of it. It was the custom to burn one effigy, that of Judas, but this time the people had decided to burn two - of us! Had we seen and heard what had been done that morning, we would have been better prepared for the events which followed in the evening. However, we remained in blissful ignorance.

We had made friends with the couple who lived next door - a telegraphist and his wife. They had agreed to our holding a meeting in their home that afternoon, so at around four o'clock we started our meeting, with five people in attendance. One of these, a hard-looking, steely-eyed man, stayed completely poker-faced throughout and left immediately the meeting ended. We learned later that this was Bernardo, a paid killer who was responsible for the two crosses down by the railway track - the place where he had killed two policemen. Evidently he had come to spy out the land, as it were. Afterwards, we went home and had supper. I went to my hammock just before nine, my run-down condition causing me to tire easily. Gordon remained in the front room, reading his Bible and praying. Suddenly he called out to me, "Jackie, I'm going for a walk - I feel I must go out." As he spoke, the still small voice within prompted me, saying "You go with him." "Wait a minute, Gordon, I'm coming too." I called.

I dressed hurriedly and joined Gordon at the front door. We turned up our road towards the main street, walking slowly because my feet hurt. We talked to the Lord as we went, asking Him what He wanted us to do. Nobody went for a walk in the evening in Brazil. There were no street lights and the roads were deserted. We walked down the main street and as we crossed over into the square we heard the voice of a priest over the loudspeaker. He was calling the people to join him in a march to the house of the Protestants. "We will show them that they are not welcome here," he said.

As we walked across the square, we suddenly heard the noise of a large crowd rushing up the main street behind us. Gordon remarked that perhaps it was a good thing that we were not at home. The people would most probably congregate in front of our house, chant and sing and then leave and at this point we would be able to return home.

Suddenly a bunch of people came running across the square to us, shouting. They started to throw pieces of rubble and stones at us. "Keep walking, Jackie," Gordon said. Stunned, I kept going. We walked on with the group right behind us until we came to the large new brick Post Office. "We'd better stop and face them," whispered Gordon. We stopped and turned. They were shouting, "Long live Mary, death to the Protestants! Long live the Queen of Heaven!" Some had their hands on their knives, as if waiting for someone to give the word to attack. "This is the end of our missionary journey," Gordon said, and took my hand. Suddenly a peace and joy invaded my being and I stood straight, smiling at the crowd in front of us. All fear had gone. "Now I know how the martyrs die," I thought. "How wonderful Jesus is - I shall see Him soon now - and Wendy."

Just at that moment, a man came out of the Post Office with a pistol in his hand. "This is it, Jackie," Gordon said. Instead of shooting us however, he pushed through the crowd, grabbed and pulled us toward the open door of the Post Office. It seemed as if the crowd had been struck immobile - they were too surprised to move! As they saw the door close on us and our rescuer stand with his back to it facing them, they ran to him with a shout. He pointed his pistol at them "This is Government property," he said. "The first one to pass that gate I'll shoot!" The crowd halted abruptly, looked at one another and at the determined attitude of the man with the pistol and slowly turned away, grumbling. The man came inside and shut and bolted the door. He smiled at us, "You can breathe now - you're safe here. I am the Chief of the Post Office. Come up to my apartment and sit down for a while."

The strength seemed to have gone from my legs and I was glad to sit down. The Chief fetched me a glass of water. The Lord had given me strength and grace for the ordeal but now I felt my weakness!

"I'm sorry about this," the Chief said. "I'm not a Christian but my parents were Presbyterians. I'm afraid that Protestants are not very welcome here, as you can see."

We spent a little time discussing the situation when suddenly there was a sharp knock on the main door. Our friend went down and opened it. When he rejoined us he was accompanied by two policemen. They greeted us courteously but stiffly. "Your house has been broken into," they said. "Everything in your house has been destroyed and there is a fire burning outside. We are very sorry." Gordon started up, "I must go back there," he said. "I'm coming too," I added firmly. "We will escort you," said the policemen. The Post Office Chief said he would join us later.

As we approached our home, we could see the fire burning

brightly. There were still many people milling around the place. Our police escort disappeared and we slowly entered the house, picking our way through the broken remains of our belongings. Everything that would burn was on the fire: Bibles, books, furniture. My mind went back to the war - the place looked as though a small bomb had exploded in it!

Gordon rummaged around in the mess on the floor. He suddenly picked something up and exclaimed, "Here's a page from my Bible," - it was John's Gospel, chapter three with verse sixteen underlined! "I am going to talk to those people out there." he said.

I watched as he stood up on a pile of rocks by the side of the fire. He stood there, holding out the torn page of Scripture. The people started to gather round and I held my breath, wondering what was going to happen. As he started to speak, I began to pray.

Gordon told the people about the first Good Friday and the words of Jesus - "Father forgive them for they know not what they do." Slowly and clearly he told them that we, too, forgave them. He read John 3:16 and, encouraged by the quiet and attentive crowd, he preached the full Gospel - of the power of Jesus to save and heal. As he finished and stepped down, the people turned to one another and I heard some say, "We are wrong, these people are not bad. We should not have treated them like this." Others remained silent but walked away slowly and thoughtfully. Gradually the crowd melted away. Somebody brought us some coffee and then our Post Office friend arrived, accompanied by a photographer. "Please let him take a picture of you in the remains of your home," he said. The photographer quickly did his job and then left. "You can't stay here for the night," Snr. Jose said, "You must come back to the Post Office and sleep there - it's the strongest building in town." As we tried to close the doors of our house, we discovered our hammocks hanging intact, behind the door. We took them down and accompanied Jose back to his apartment. "We will sleep now and talk things over in the morning," he said. We rolled into our hammocks and fell asleep, worn out by the strain of the evening's events.

TWENTY-FIVE

"FERVENT PRAYER WAS PERSISTENTLY MADE TO GOD" ACTS 12:5

Early the next morning, we got up, feeling stiff. Some of the pieces of rubble had given us a few bruises. As we drank our coffee, prepared by Jose, we discussed our position. Our friend had been going round, finding out about the attack on us. He told us what had happened. It appeared that they had made the Police Captain drunk, so that at the time of the attack he was incapable of directing his men, who had been afraid to interfere without his authority.

The Priest was the ringleader, with several other leading citizens backing him up. Among them was the lawyer husband of the lady I had met! They had hired a paid killer - Bernardo - to make sure the job was done. The leaders were really angry because their plan had failed but thought that we would be too scared to stay in town after what had happened. Periodically, the Priest shouted out threats over the loudspeakers, declaring what they would do to us when they found us!

Jose marvelled that we had both not been at home when the attack took place. "You would both have been killed, for sure, if you had remained in the house." he said. We told him how the Holy Spirit had spoken to both of us to leave the property, just five minutes before the crowd arrived. "It must have been God!" he said. "But this is not the end of the matter, you know. These people are fanatical in their religion and will never let you stay here," he said. We told him that the very fact that God had saved us from death that night was a sign that He wanted us here.

Jose shook his head slowly. "I'm glad that the angels are

taking care of you," he said, "You don't know what you are up against." How much the Lord had done to save us, even we didn't know at that time. However, five years later, when we went on furlough, we learned more about His wonderful rescue operation. While visiting two friends who had been at Lynton with us, they produced a diary and opened it at the date of the Good Friday attack on us. "What happened that night?" they asked. "We were awakened at about two o'clock in the morning and the Lord asked us to pray for you as you were in danger. For two hours we prayed, until the burden was lifted from us and we felt you were safe!"

We told our friends about the events that took place on that night. Owing to the difference in time, the hour at which they were wakened coincided with the beginning of the attack on us. As the realization of what had happened dawned on us all, we started praising God and went into a wonderful time of worship. How thankful we were that our friends had been obedient to the Holy Spirit! Who knows how the matter might have ended had they not been obedient!

That Saturday morning after the attack, we were unaware of all this as we sat over coffee and considered our situation. Snr. Jose said we must go to Fortaleza and report the matter to the authorities, - but how? All our money had been stolen, together with my engagement ring that had belonged to my mother. Snr. Jose said that he could let us have enough for one ticket but that, as it was the end of the month, he was low on funds until pay day. Whatever happened, he said, Gordon must go to the coast.

A single-track railway line ran from Missao Velha to Fortaleza. The train, one of the early, wood-burning types, came in once a week, stayed for two hours and then returned. It had just come in that morning. Gordon said, "What can I do about my wife? I can't leave her alone here, Snr. Jose!"

As we talked a lady came in. It was the lawyer's wife, whom I had met during my walk that week. She was really indignant - "I will never set foot in the church again!" she said. "I can't understand my husband being a part of that cowardly attack. He is without shame! What can I do to help you?" she asked. We explained the position to her. "I haven't enough money to pay Dona Jacquelina's fare to the coast, but I will take her home with me and care for her while Snr. Estevao is away." Gordon looked at her aghast. "With your husband against us - how can you take my wife home with you? What will your husband do?" he asked. Snra. Maria da Fatima looked at him calmly. "The laws of hospitality are very strong in Brazil," she said, "Once your wife is under our roof my husband will not touch her or allow anybody else to do so."

Gordon and I were silent, both considering the possibility of my living for an indefinite period in the house of a fanatic, in a community of people out for our blood! I could see that my husband didn't like the idea, but none of us could come up with an alternative. It was Snr. Jose who settled the matter. "Thank you, Snra. Fatima," he said. "I'm sure that Dona Jacquelina will be safe with you, especially when your husband learns that I know she is with you! Don't let her put a foot out of the house, whatever happens." Gordon looked at me and said, "How do you feel about this, Jackie?" My sense of humour came to the fore, and I replied, "If God can shut the mouths of lions and keep Daniel alive in their den, I'm sure He can look after me. God is in this and He won't fail us."

Snr. Jose was obviously relieved and began briefing Gordon as to whom he should contact on his arrival in Fortaleza. Gordon said that he would seek out the Pentecostal church there first of all, as he knew that the brethren would help him, and as soon as he could he would send money for me to join him.

The clang of the train bell interrupted our conversation so Gordon bade us a quick farewell and ran to the railway station nearby. A few minutes later we heard the train making its noisy departure. Snra. Fatima turned to me and said that we had better be going. Her husband was out and would not return until lunch time. I thanked Snr Jose again and left the Post Office with Snra Fatima. We went through the back streets to her house, happily not meeting anybody. As soon as we entered her house, Fatima shut the window-shutters so that no one could see me.

Her sixteen-year-old son was the first to come home. His eyes widened in astonishment on seeing me - the English 'protestant' was in his home! His mother spoke sharply and told him what she expected of him. He was obviously an obedient son but I could see that he wasn't quite sure how he should behave towards me. Fatima soon made that clear and thereafter I was treated with great respect. When lunchtime arrived, I could see that Fatima was becoming nervous, in anticipation of her husband's arrival. After all, it was no light thing to defy her husband in such a matter!

Snr. Almeida arrived, washed his hands and came straight to the dining table, where I was already seated with Roberto, the son. He gave one look at me and strode into the kitchen, banging the door behind him. After a few minutes he returned and if looks could kill I would have died right then! However, he sat down, unfolded his napkin and without a further look at me, proceeded to eat a hearty meal. My own hunger overcame my nervous reaction and I, too, gave my attention to the good food. We all ate in silence. After the dessert, Snr. Almeida got up and went to the front 'sala', beckoning his son to join him, where his wife served coffee to them. She was very subdued but something about the set of her chin showed her determination. Snr. Almeida did not say one word to me during the whole time I was there but I had several conversations with Roberto, the son. The situation intrigued him - all this fuss over one solitary pair of English Protestants!

The priest was still making announcements over the loudspeakers three times a day, threatening and promising dire consequences when Gordon and I were found. He said that the 'valentoes' - brave men - of nearby towns were joining them in their campaign against us. Roberto obviously felt that such an outcry was ludicrous. Here was an ordinary woman who didn't even speak very good Brazilian and her husband who couldn't be anybody very special, either, and yet his fellow townsmen were going to all lengths to get rid of them! What was it they taught that made the people so mad against them? A very intelligent lad, he asked many questions and his mother sat by, listening to our conversation. She was growing more nervous each time the priest spoke and her husband's face was becoming darker and darker as time went on.

Back in my bedroom, I sought the Lord. In spite of everything, I had His peace in my heart. I hated to feel, however, that I was causing trouble for my kind benefactress. "Please get me out of this, Lord, and heal the division between Fatima and her husband" I prayed. Don't let their marriage suffer because of her bravery. Open his eyes to the truth." It was now two days since I had come to their home, and I could see that poor Fatima was near breaking point. In desperation I cried out to the Lord!

TWENTY-SIX

"JUAZEIRO DO NORTE"

Unbeknown to us, the American Baptists who were living about four hours' drive away, had heard of our coming to Missao Velha. They knew nothing about the attack on us but had decided to pay us a neighbourly visit.

Their Jeep came slowly up the street as they looked for someone to ask the whereabouts of the English couple. On seeing a lady walking towards them, they stopped and asked her if she knew where the English people lived. Once she realized who they were she poured out the story of the attack on us and urged them to take me away with them. Yes, of all the people they might have met, our American brethren had come upon my hostess! They listened, bewildered, to the torrent of words pouring from this agitated lady. When she finally stopped, they asked her to get in the Jeep and guide them to her house. Fortunately, her husband was not in and so, over coffee, I told our visitors what had happened. Jim and David listened quietly, but as I finished, Fatima broke in again, once more urging them to take me away immediately. Jim told me to get my things ready, which took me no time at all, as I had nothing to take with me!

Fatima was so relieved and cried as I embraced her to say good-bye. I thanked her for her kindness and bravery and told her that I hoped to see her again soon. At that, she cried all the harder and told me that we must never return! The priest and his followers had become really worked up again and there was no knowing what they would do if we dared to show ourselves openly in the place!

We drove quietly out of town towards Juazeiro do Norte. Jim and Dave discussed the situation with me. They said that they felt that the attack on us might spark off an offensive against all the missionaries in that large area. Besides themselves and their families, there was one other couple and a single lady who lived in Juazeiro, and another family who lived in a town several hours' journey away. So few against so many!

Juazeiro had a curious history and Jim and Dave shared with me a little of what they had learned. It was a large town of some fifty thousand inhabitants. There was a nucleus of brick-built houses and shops that had been built around the high, imposing church, which was surrounded by hundreds of small mud huts. A large monastery, inhabited by Italian Franciscan monks dominated the town and they also had their own church on the outskirts. A priest by the name of Padre Cicero had died there a few years previously, after a most strange life. He had unusual powers and the people from miles around almost worshiped him - even to that day. Obviously he was a spiritist, because he could throw his hat at the wall and it would stay there, and move tables by just touching them. His powers of healing especially had made him a man of renown. The Catholic church had excommunicated him but that had caused the people to revolt. They founded a settlement, with their own 'holy family' centering around Padre Cicero, and became a law unto themselves. Finally, the government had to send the military and even drop a bomb, in order to bring the people into submission!

The house where P. Cicero had lived was kept as a shrine to his memory. Crutches, plaster casts of legs, arms and even heads, filled the place, to commemorate his healings. Pieces of his cassock were sold, to be infused in hot water and the liquid drunk to cure sicknesses! He must have been a giant, for the material to be still available!

Many of the people made their living from making and selling little busts and figurines of his likeness. Before he died, the Padre had said he would come back one day, and when business got slack, the merchants published leaflets and distributed them, reminding people of his expected return! A wave of religious fervour would then sweep over the town and business would once again prosper!

The American Mid-West Baptists had a small Bible School in Juazeiro. Jim and Dave had been there for several years but had to move very cautiously and as yet they only had a few members in their little church. We eventually arrived at their compound, enclosed within high walls. When the gates were shut, we all felt isolated and safe from the superstitious practices of this strange town, especially when, once a year, a pilgrimage was made by thousands of people to P. Cicero's shrine. The pilgrims came by the truckload camping in the street, gypsy fashion, for a couple of days.

I was introduced to Evelyn, Jim's wife, and their little son. The spacious home was cool and for the first time in three days I felt I could relax. As soon as they saw the ulcers on my legs and feet, they took me to the doctor, who prescribed the necessary treatment. The food was simple but good, and I was given vitamins. They had a kerosene cooking-stove with an oven and a kerosene refrigerator. I slept in a big, comfortable bed - this was heaven!

We dispatched a telegram to Gordon, informing him of where I was staying. A couple of days later I was visited by some reporters, who had somehow discovered my whereabouts and were interested in meeting me, having heard what happened in Missao Velha. The story got into seven newspapers, two with a nationwide coverage.

My new friends bought me some material and a dressmaker quickly ran up a few clothes for me to wear. Living quietly with these kind people, my health rapidly improved. There was one thing which hurt me a lot. Dave and his wife Mabel had a dear little blonde daughter the same age as Wendy, who was so like her! Mabel would bring her over nearly every afternoon and as I watched her play, a sword would pierce my heart and I would have to go to my room and cry.

Photo taken of Jackie & Gordon just after the attack on their home in Missao Velha, Good Friday, 1952.

Wood-burning train - Single track from Grato to Fortaleza.

The "House of Miracles" - Padre Cicero's home, kept to commemorate him as a centre for yearly pilgrimages by his followers.

Gordon taking out the tooth of a bandit's daughter and also teaching fellow missionary, Eduardo.

Preparing corn to make corn bread. Vicente's wife and family.

A baptismal service held during the draught.

Vicente, a new creature in Christ. Taken in the yard of his home.

Part of congregation in a tent meeting.

Our band in the tent meeting.

The "Hour of Decision" after a meeting in the Hall at Bragança Pancista.

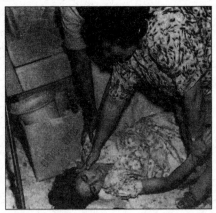

Woman delivered from demon possession after eight years, with Pedrinha, a woman helper.

A baptismal service in the interior - we had to dig the hole!

One of the church groups in an out-station of Bragança Paulista.

Taken just before moving to Portugal 1965.

Eduardo, Alberto &, behind, Gordon on one of their journeys into the interior of Pariaifa.

The 'laundry' at a river during the draught.

Two men died & were buried in this country place.

TWENTY-SEVEN

"THE LAW OF MAN OR THE LAW OF GOD"

The days slipped by without any news from Gordon. Then about after three weeks, Gordon returned. He told us all about his visit to Fortaleza and how he had found his way to the house of the Pastor of the Assembly of God. Brother Teixeira had been an illiterate, backward boy, but he had come to the town and preached the Gospel, earning his living by tailoring. He learned to read and write and his fervour and fearlessness soon began to attract many of the people to his meetings. The church grew until, by the time of Gordon's visit, it had reached several thousand members in the town and surrounding suburbs, from all walks of life.

Dark-skinned and short, Bro. Teixeira was afraid of nobody. On one occasion, when a Brazilian preacher had been subjected to persecution in an interior town, Teixeira had taken a truck-load of believers there. He had stood on the truck, facing the crowds that gathered, holding a Bible in one hand and a gun in the other. "Which one do you people want - the law of the land or the law of God? You've broken the law of the land, in doing harm to our brothers. Do you want me to bring in the police or will you listen to and obey the Gospel of Jesus Christ?" he thundered. He then preached for half an hour - there was no more trouble in that town!

When he heard Gordon's story he was indignant. To think that his fellow-countrymen should treat a brother in Christ, and an Englishman at that, in such a way really upset him! When he heard that Gordon had only the clothes he stood up in, our dear brother took his measurements, hunted out some material and stayed up all night making him a suit! The next day he telephoned his son-in-law, a lawyer, and together they discussed their plan of action. It was decided that Gordon should first of all go to the Police, then to the

Roman Catholic Bishop, accompanied by the lawyer. Our British Consul had also been notified.

They were received courteously by the Chief of Police, who informed him that the government was having trouble enforcing the law in the interior towns, where the people gave priority to the orders of the Priest. However, he couldn't deny that the law of Brazil gave equal rights to both Catholic and Protestant, and said he would send orders to Missao Velha and Juazeiro do Norte, telling the police there to protect us. They would do all they could to make the people understand that they could no longer kill and hurt people in the name of religion, and that, if and when they did, the perpetrators of such crimes would suffer the consequences.

The Bishop graciously extended his hand to be kissed and Gordon shook it. The prelate explained that he had little control in the interior as they had their own Bishop, who had his seat in the city of Crato - half an hour from Juazeiro. "The interior people are very ignorant and backward," he remarked, "and very hot blooded - I advise you to stay on the coast." Gordon realized that little could be hoped for in that direction and took his leave. He knew it was no good telling the Bishop that it was largely the fault of the Catholic church that the people were so ignorant!

Unfortunately, our Consul was away, and so Gordon had to see his assistant, who as good as told him that it was his own fault if he got into trouble, since he shouldn't interfere with the people's religion! Gordon left before he lost his temper! When the English community who lived in Fortaleza heard of our experience, however, they kindly sent us a gift of money.

Gordon and Teixeira had great fellowship together. The Pastor admired people who would brave the rigors of life in the interior for the sake of the Gospel. We were people after his own heart, and he told Gordon that he had only to call and he would come with a truck-load of believers and show those people in Missao Velha that they couldn't push the believers around! However, we never did call upon him - we felt we should use different tactics.

TWENTY-EIGHT

"MAN PROPOSES, GOD DISPOSES"

Once Gordon was back we held a 'council of war' with the Baptists. What was to be our next step? Someone had to go and live in Missao Velha or our adversaries would try out these violent attacks on other missionaries, thinking that they would get rid of us all that way. Gordon insisted that as the Lord had called him and me to that town, we must go back! The point was, how were we to get back?

We purposed to return to Missao Velha in a week's time. However, the day before we were due to leave, we received a telegram from an anonymous source, warning us against returning at that time. Gordon doubted the motives of the sender - "They're trying to scare us off," he said, "we are going, anyway!" However 'man proposes, God disposes'. We went to the station to catch the one and only train, only to see it disappearing round a bend in the track! Gordon was really upset. "We'll go by truck, then," he suggested, but try as he would, he couldn't find anybody going to Missao Velha! With Gordon fuming, we returned to the Baptist School. The next day we had a visitor, the man who had sent the telegram, it transpired.

Snr. Valdemar told us how the priests were anticipating our attempts to return to Missao Velha. The day before, the Priest, together with all the young student priests from the Seminary, and crowds of people from the town, had waited at the station with bags of stones and fireworks, and carrying banners. A really warm reception was planned but the Lord had prevented our return and Gordon had to admit it! We certainly kept the angels who were assigned to our case busy!

However, our return to Missao Velha had to be attempted. Gordon told the Police Colonel in Juazeiro that we were determined to go back, but he told us that he could not allow us to go alone as he had orders to protect us. It was finally decided that on the first trip, Jim and Gordon should go, escorted by fifty policemen and the Colonel. The police, by the way, also served as soldiers in the army.

When the day came for the visit, we committed everyone to the Lord and watched as they all boarded the bus. The Colonel and two men went by Jeep. On their arrival, the Colonel stood with Jim and Gordon in the center of the town square with the police surrounding them. As Jim had started to speak, there was a stir up at the far end of the main street, and minutes later a crowd started to form and move down the street. First came the Priest, then the Daughters and Sons of Mary, followed by the rest of the people, all singing "Ave Maria" as they walked.

When Jim had finished speaking, it was Gordon's turn. He looked around at the soldiers and up at the approaching crowd. The Colonel gave the order to fix bayonets but this did not deter the crowd from coming on down. Gordon started to speak, assuring the people that they had come in peace and only wanted to be allowed to return and live amicably in the town but it was impossible - the noise of the singing drowned him! Suddenly a man darted forward, slipping through the police cordon. He fell on his knees in front of Gordon. "Senhor, senhor, please stop and go away. Blood will be shed if you don't!" Gordon assured him that was the last thing he wanted. "Who are you?" he asked the man. "I am the Mayor," he said. "Well then, promise that you will talk to the Priest and the others and quieten them down, so we can come back and live here. I won't go until you promise you will do that." Gordon said. "I promise, I promise, senhor, but please go now," he pleaded.

Jim and the Colonel had heard this conversation and the Colonel took the Mayor aside and spoke to him. Suddenly he ordered the men to put down their rifles and follow Jim and Gordon back into the bus. Then he and his two officers went off in his Jeep, the bus following. A roar went up from the crowd and they let off the usual fireworks as a sign of victory! Within a few days we had a note from the Police Chief, saying that we could now return to Missao Velha.

Taking with us the good wishes of the Baptists, we boarded the train back home. As we left the station and made our way up the main street, curious glances were thrown at us by some of the bystanders. When we entered our house, we found everything as we had left it - the floors covered with the debris of broken china, crushed pans and torn up clothes. We started on the grim task of cleaning up and repairing the locks on the doors. We had managed to obtain some packing-cases which we used as furniture.

Two of our neighbours who ran a little corner shop, were surprisingly friendly. They had been shocked by the happenings on the Good Friday. As we discussed the events of that night, the wife, Maria da Lua said, "You know, if your baby had been with you, you wouldn't have gone out so late at night, would you? God took your baby to heaven so that your life might be spared. He must have some special work for you to do!" As I settled into my hammock that night, I pondered over her words. That must be another reason why the Lord took Wendy. Dona Lua was right - I would have probably ignored that small voice within me, urging me to accompany Gordon that night. The killer would have been enraged at not finding Gordon and certainly wouldn't have spared Wendy and me!

About four days later, after we had just about got the place cleaned and repaired, a small bomb was thrown into our backyard. It didn't do much damage, however, - just made more mess! There was a man in town who made fireworks for a living, and it was he who had made the bomb, we learned later. He made another bigger bomb, also intended for us, but something went wrong and it exploded, blasting him up into a nearby tree, where he died a painful death. The Brazilians came and told us about this, and other things that had happened to some of those who attacked us. The Priest himself had suddenly developed tuberculosis and been sent to the

Sanatorium by the Bishop. One man had gone blind while yet another went mad and so on. These reports saddened us and we assured these messengers of evil tidings that we only wished their people well, not harm. They however, shook their heads and said that it was the judgment of God upon them.

Two more weeks passed by, uneventfully. Since the death of the firework-maker, no more attacks had been made on us. Gordon succeeded in renting a small room on the outskirts of town, for holding meetings. We had to walk through some narrow lanes in order to get to it and I couldn't help but think that this would afford our enemies an opportunity to harm us. I remembered the promise of God, "No weapon forged against you will prevail and you will refute every tongue that accuses you." Isaiah 54:17. We had certainly seen the fulfillment of this verse already - what more proof did I require or assurance that God's angels were watching over us!

TWENTY-NINE

"LAY HANDS ON THE SICK AND THEY
SHALL RECOVER" MARK 16:18

The day before we were due to start the meetings, a man called at our house. I opened the door and there stood Bernardo, the killer! He told us that his son was dying of a high fever which the doctor had been unable to cure. He remembered hearing Gordon saying that "Jesus is the same, yesterday, today, and forever," and that He still heals the sick. He asked Gordon if he would go and pray for his little son.

Naturally, I was a little hesitant over this but Gordon said he must go, adding that if he wasn't back in an hour I was to go to the Police. As he left the house with Bernardo I got down to prayer. Within the hour he returned, really excited and praising God. He told me that when he had reached Bernardo's home, they had indeed found the child lying in his hammock, dying. The candles were all lit around him, and the family were weeping. Gordon realized that a great deal depended on the healing of this child. As he laid his hands on the boy's head which was burning with fever, he reminded the Lord of this before rebuking the sickness in the Name of Jesus and claiming complete healing for the boy. He then stood back, by the side of Bernardo, and watched the little boy. The mother and family stopped their wailing and were also watching. Gordon could feel the tension mounting in Bernardo.

Suddenly the boy raised his head and asked for water. He sat up slowly and drank eagerly, then said, "I'm hungry, give me my supper." The mother, overjoyed rushed to prepare some rice gruel for him.

Bernardo, watched, fascinated as the boy took the gruel and then got out of the hammock and started playing on the floor. "What are all the candles for?" he asked. His big sister blew them out, tears running down her face. Bernardo suddenly came to life and grabbed his son in his arms. "The fever's gone!" he shouted as he kissed him. Putting the bewildered boy down, he turned to Gordon. "Thank you," he said simply. "From now on I will always be your friend and nobody shall touch you. I will be your guard whenever you go out at night." Gordon quietly thanked him but told him that we did not need his protection. "Who do you think saved us on Good Friday?" he asked. Bernardo was silent for a moment, then said, "You don't know my people, senhor." "You don't know my God!" was Gordon's reply. After reminding the family that it was Jesus who had healed the boy, not him, and telling them of His love and pardon, Gordon left.

No wonder that Gordon was excited! God had turned one of our worst enemies into our friend and would-be protector! The impact of this on the town was tremendous. Unfortunately, others who had been among the ring-leaders did not change in the same way.

When Bernardo heard that we were going to start having meetings, he arrived at our house on the first night, just as we were leaving home. He insisted on following behind us until we arrived at the meeting-place and then, instead of coming in he remained outside, hidden in the shadows. At the end of the meeting, he again followed us home, bidding us a courteous goodnight as we entered our house. He did this for the next few weeks. Some of the braver souls started coming to the meeting and a few accepted Jesus as their Saviour. Several were healed of various diseases.

One day we were asked to visit a man who was dying from T.B. He was black and had once been a strong and fine-looking man, employed as a porter at the railway station. When we saw him he was mere skin and bones, lying in his little hut and coughing his life out. His family were gathered sadly round him, not expecting him to last much longer. We laid hands on him and ordered that terrible disease to leave, in the Name of Jesus. After praying with the family, we gave them some money to buy food and then left.

Our next meeting was held four days later and we made our way there, with Bernardo behind us, as usual. This particular evening we had a special visitor - the black porter for whom we had prayed! Tall and gaunt, he walked in slowly, but it was obvious that the Lord had performed a miracle! About ten days later he returned to his job at the railway, carrying heavy loads on his head! The healing caused a stir in the town, with the result that more people came to the Saviour for salvation and healing.

Strangely enough, this manifestation of the power of God seemed to rouse our enemies to fresh outbursts of persecution against the small body of believers! Several lost their jobs and decided to leave town. Others found it difficult to buy food and do business. Even some of the children had been taught to follow us and "baa" behind us, like sheep. One day, Gordon, tired of this constant harassment pulled out a handful of corn from his pocket and scattered it in front of the children saying, "There you are, poor hungry things!" This took them aback and they soon tired of that pastime!

THIRTY

"LOVE YOUR ENEMIES" MATTHEW 5:44

A short time after our return to Missao Velha, Gordon had to go to visit the main bank in Crato, a city about three hours journey away by train. This city was a busy centre upon which converged four states, being the hub of the commerce of the area. It was also the site of the colleges and seat of the Bishop, while the paper 'Catholic Action' had its headquarters there as well. A large new hospital had been recently built on the outskirts.

It was necessary for Gordon to go there once a month, in order to get our remittance from the Bank. On this, his first visit, he met the manager, who was excited when he discovered that Gordon was English. "Please will you come and teach us English?" he asked. "Many of us have studied your language in the course of our education but we need someone who can teach us the correct pronunciation and advanced English. Will you come and help us?" Gordon explained that he didn't really have the time but that he would ask his wife if she would teach them! The manager promised that they would take great care of me. Obviously very embarrassed, he referred to the attack on us, and said that of course it had shocked the more enlightened people of the city! Gordon said that if I took classes in Crato it would necessitate my spending a night there. The Manager immediately called in his Chief clerk, Snr. Neri, and with much enthusiasm told him about the proposed English class. The clerk agreed to make all the arrangements and offered the hospitality of his home. We discovered later that he held a high office in the Catholic church!

Gordon returned home very pleased with the outcome of his

visit. The English class would bring in some much-needed finances as well as helping us make some friends in the area. He told me where I would be spending the night, and commented that they would certainly be keeping an eye on me, in more ways than one. Although I was only a woman, they weren't taking any chances by letting me loose in the city! As for me, I faced my first visit to Crato with some trepidation. My knowledge of the intricacies of the English language was fairly good, so I wasn't very worried on that account, but once again I seemed to be going into the lion's den! It was taking me time to realize that they were muzzled! The 'Catholic Action' newspaper had printed some rather poisonous articles about us and the citizens were known for their religious fervor. Our Baptist friends had told us of attacks that had been made on the Bible bookstall they had attempted to set up in the local market.

A few days before I went to Crato to hold my first class, Gordon went off on one of his regular trips to an outpost he had set up in the surrounding countryside. He planned to be away for a few days. It was arranged that a young woman, one of our converts, would stay with me while he was away.

While I was sitting reading one evening, the local priest came to my mind. I had heard that he had recently returned from the sanatorium, where he had spent some weeks, and I felt a strong urge to pay him a visit. Knowing this 'urge' to be of the Holy Spirit, I asked my young companion if she knew where the Priest lived, and if she would accompany me to his house. Lourdes looked at me in astonishment, as I told her I felt I should visit him, but added she needn't go in with me. It was agreed that she stay with a believer who lived nearby while I was at the Priest's house, and then I could pick her up when I left.

We committed ourselves to the Lord and set off along the dark streets. When we arrived at the Priest's house, I told Lourdes to ask the believers to pray for me. She then left and I knocked on the door. It opened, rather cautiously, and I found myself face to face with the priest himself. We looked at each other in mutual astonishment - he at seeing the English woman on his doorstep and I at encountering a short, skinny young man with a thin, pale face - so different from how I imagined he would look.

He obviously didn't know what to say to me, and I was moved with compassion for this inarticulate young man. How different from the eloquent speaker who had stirred the blood of the people with his impassioned tirades against the Protestants! I inquired after his health and asked if he had fully recovered from his sickness. He thanked me for my visit and concern and then just sat and looked at me wonderingly. I made a few remarks, which I don't even remember now, and then rose to leave. He again thanked me for my visit and showed me to the door. I collected Lourdes and we returned home. Short though my visit had been, I had a sense of having done all the Lord required of me that night.

Before I went to my hammock later on, I prayed for the young priest and our persecutors. The love of God, which He had poured into my heart, went out to them. I realized in a new way that we were not battling against flesh and blood but against the spiritual powers of darkness in high places that had blinded these poor people.

THIRTY-ONE

"A WIDE DOOR OF EFFECTUAL SERVICE
HAS OPENED TO ME" I CORINTHIANS 16:9

The day arrived for my visit to Crato to take my first English class. I repeated the following Scripture to myself several times - "I can do all things through Christ who strengthens me," - giving emphasis to different words each time. Fortified by the Word I set out to catch the train.

I was met at the station by a young woman called Maria da Carma. She explained that she and her sister-in-law Conçeiçáo lived with Snr. Neri and his wife, Serafina. She herself was a student who stayed in Crato while studying, as her home was too far away for her to commute daily to the college she attended. Conçeiçáo helped Serafina, while hoping to find a husband. Her prospects were better in Crato than in the village where her family lived. It transpired that Carma was a Daughter of Mary, which explained her cool attitude toward me.

When I arrived I was welcomed by Serafina, who appeared to be a simple-hearted and kindly woman. She told us that lunch was almost ready and her husband would soon be home. The presence of the son of the house, a dear chubby little boy of eight months helped lighten the atmosphere - I could see that the natural friendliness of my hostess was curbed by the fact that Carma was with us. I was glad when Snr. Neri arrived and greeted me in English.

Serafina hastened to set the meal on the table, helped by Conçeiçáo, who was a rather insipid young woman. The cook went home. As I ate the good food set before me, Snr. Neri chatted away and I marvelled at his grasp of the English language. His pronunciation was strange and conjugation of verbs was often incorrect but, after all, he had never met an English person in his life, neither did he have any records or cassettes to listen to. How he enjoyed having an English person to talk to, even if only a woman! Although Brazilian women were expected to obey their lord and master's every whim, foreign women were treated with great respect!

After lunch and an afternoon rest, my host told me about the class which was to take place in his house after supper. It would consist of two doctors, the Bank Manager, four Bank clerks, a lawyer, a business man and a teacher who was also a priest! He looked at me a little nervously and I tried not to show my surprise, as he hurriedly explained that Padre Montenegro was a real gentleman from a very good family, and he was the right hand man of the Bishop. The last piece of information didn't exactly calm my nervousness! Neri went on to say that he was the head of the seminary of priests and taught advanced English in the colleges. The situation was getting worse and worse!

Later that evening, my pupils began to arrive and seated themselves around the large dining-table. Everyone seemed very affable and on good terms with one another. Some shook hands with me, others took my hand and kissed it or just bowed to me. It was not the custom for men to shake hands with women and they didn't know how they should greet an English woman.

Finally, they were all in their places except for the priest. Suddenly he made his appearance. Tall, and a commanding personage, his presence had a subduing effect on the others. Padre Montenegro was introduced to me and made a stiff little bow. Then we all settled down to our lesson.

As they were all in different stages in their studies, I could see it was going to be rather difficult to teach them all together as one class, and suggested that we divide up into two groups. This suggestion was met with approval and I made the division as tactfully as I could. However, their ideas on this differed from mine, and I found that only three of them, Neri and two very serious Bank clerks wanted to be in the advanced section with the priest. I discovered later that they were all Sons of Mary.

By the end of the class I had begun to feel more at ease. I was encouraged that they were anxious to learn and that the first group especially, seemed really willing to be friendly. This was a welcome change after the strained relations prevailing between us and so many of the Missao Velha townspeople.

When they had all gone home, Levi talked with me for a while and then we went to our hammocks. Carma, the sister-in-law, shared her room with me and I had noticed she was beginning to thaw out a little. No doubt the presence of the priest had influenced her attitude toward me.

P. Montenegro had been reserved but not unfriendly to me. In fact he had been the last to go and had drawn me aside before he left. "I trust you do not mind me attending your classes," he said, "I must explain that I abhor the way you were treated in Missao Velha and I hope that you will forgive the ignorance of my people. My colleagues are against me studying with you but, as I have to teach advanced English, it is imperative that I improve my knowledge of your language." I realized that it was no easy thing for this proud man to speak as he did, and my heart warmed to him. I assured him that Gordon and I had forgiven the attackers and only wished to prove our goodwill toward him and his people. I added that I would do all I could to help him with his studies.

I slept well that night and awoke early to see Carma slipping out of the room. The regulations governing the Daughters and Sons of Mary were demanding in their insistence upon strict religious observances. Attendance at early morning Mass, all the religious services and feasts were obligatory.

We had a pleasant breakfast, with Neri talking and asking questions most of the time. I liked the little man, with his witticisms and thirst for knowledge. He seemed to like me, too, and was anxious to explain Brazilian customs. He also helped me with some of the difficulties I was having with the Brazilian language.

After breakfast, I was duly escorted to the station and boarded the train. As I got on at one end, I was surprised to see P. Levi from Missao Velha getting on at the other!

THIRTY-TWO

A REQUEST FOR FORGIVENESS

We were travelling noisily away from the city, when the priest came into my compartment. When he realized that I was alone, he came and sat beside me. He explained that he had been to make his monthly report to the Bishop. I told him about my English class, mentioning casually that P. Montenegro was one of my pupils, which really shook him! We talked about the terrible drought which had caused such distress in the land, and the time passed quickly. Soon the train started to slow down as we approached our destination. P. Levi got up, and said good-bye and left the compartment. I took the hint and when we got off the train we ignored one another.

This was the first of several conversations as we met on the train. On about the third occasion he told me, haltingly, that he was very sorry for what he had done on that bad 'Good Friday'.

Surprised and really touched, I assured him of our forgiveness, bringing out the Gospel in its purity and simplicity. He listened attentively. When we met again, it was easier to talk to him about the Lord. He conveyed to me however, that there were still a number of people in Missao Velha who harboured a fanatical hatred toward us. He was in a difficult position and I felt sorry for him.

A few weeks after the start of our classes, P. Montenegro drew me aside after class, one evening, and said, "I'm going to your town tomorrow morning. May I have the pleasure of taking you home?" I accepted his kind offer with alacrity.

The next day he duly arrived in a beautiful highly-polished black car, which he told me was a gift from his family. There were some astonished glances from people on the pavement as we drove out of Crato!

As we sped towards Missao Velha, we talked about general topics. On arrival, we drove up the main street, where people thronged the pavements, as it was market day, and my companion slowed down. Curious looks were directed toward the beautiful car and its occupants! At the top of the street, which was the busiest part, P. Montenegro stopped the car. Slowly getting out he walked around and opened my door, politely handing me out. He shook my hand, said good-bye and returned unhurriedly to his seat. He then turned the car and drove off toward the church. I noticed with amazement the open mouths and looks of astonishment on the faces of the bystanders, and mentally took my hat off to the priest!

The next week, P. Montenegro again remained after class. This time he had a theological book with him and suggested that we sit down and have a talk. I noted that this did not altogether meet with Neri's approval, who wasn't invited to join us. We spent an interesting half-hour - the priest telling me of certain doctrines of the church and I pointing out relevant Scriptures from my Bible. From that time on, every week we had our talk after class, Neri hovering in the background, getting more and more anxious. Padre Montenegro was not put off however, and we covered some interesting ground in these talks, concerning the great truths of salvation, and I could see interest mounting in the priest.

THIRTY-THREE

*"HE MAKES EVEN HIS ENEMIES TO BE AT
PEACE WITH HIM" PROV 16:7*

Life in Missao Velha had its amusing incidents. On one occasion, a poor family - some of our first converts - got into financial difficulties, and came to us for help. At that time, we ourselves had reached the bottom of the barrel, so to speak, as it was the end of the month, so I asked the Lord what I could do. As I hunted around the almost bare shelves, I checked on what I had left - some flour, margarine, eggs and a little vanilla flavouring - enough ingredients to make quite a lot of cakes! By this time I had a tiny tin oven that could be placed on top of my charcoal fire.

The next morning, I was up at 4:30 and started baking. By the time the husband Serafino came at 8:30, I had a large batch of little cakes for him to sell. All that day I cooked and perspired over that little oven. The cakes sold well and Serafino was jubilant at the money we were making! In the late afternoon I baked a large cake and sent it out, then I used the remaining flour to make the last one - the biggest and best! As I took it out of the oven, the siren sounded, indicating the end of the working day. Serafino appeared and I handed him the cake. "This is the last one," I said. "Oh no, senhora, the siren has gone - I don't work any more today! he protested. In vain I tried to persuade him but it was no good. I took some of the money from the cakes sold to replenish the food I'd used and was able to give Serafino a handsome day's wage. I sadly regarded my 'pièce de résistance' and decided to cut it up and share it with my neighbours.

Gordon spent regular periods away from home, visiting outlying villages. On one occasion he was on such a trip, journeying on the back of a lorry in company with some other travellers. They stopped at a primitive lodging-house for the night, and relaxed for a short time while waiting for "jantar' to be served. The men fixed a target on to a tree and started shooting at it, seeing which of them was the best. After a few minutes, thinking to have some fun at Gordon's expense, they asked him to have a try, knowing that he didn't carry a gun. One of the men offered him his gun, saying "Come on, galego (foreigner), let's see what you can do!" The men laughed as Gordon quietly took the gun. To the astonishment of all present, he hit the bull's eye with his first shot! Everybody treated him with great respect after that!

Soon the call came to come to the table, which was half of a big tree that had been split down the middle. At one end sat an evil-looking woman, who started speaking in a low, tense voice to the anxious-looking man at her side. Gordon, seated at the other end of the table, sensed in his spirit that she was a practitioner of black magic, and prayed silently as he ate, binding the power that she was obviously trying to exercise over the men. The woman cast furious looks at him from time to time. Finally she stood up and pointed to Gordon. "That man has more power than I have!" she shouted, and left the table. The man to whom she had been speaking came to Gordon after the meal and asked if he could help him. After listening to his problems, Gordon told him the plan of salvation and had the joy of leading him to the Saviour before they retired to their hammocks.

The situation in Missao Vehla was not good. As fast as they came to know the Lord as their Saviour, the believers had to leave town because of persecution. Many stores refused to sell food to them. The black porter, so miraculously healed, had to leave with his family. The only ones who stayed on were Serafino and his wife Alicia, who was expecting their third child, and they hadn't enough money to start anew in another place. Poor Serafino hadn't much initiative and 'go'. Alicia came from quite a good family and had eloped with him but he didn't prove to be a very good provider for the family.

We had been in Missao Velha for a year but now we prayerfully considered leaving. Juazeiro was a large city and no real evangelistic work was being done in the place. One of our Christian families had gone there to live and they urged us to join them and start a work in the 'shanty' area on the outskirts of the town.

Rather reluctantly we packed our few possessions. In spite of the difficulties and the persecution we had been through, we had grown to like the place and, in a way, it seemed as though we were quitting the battle. Many people who had never come to our meetings, expressed sorrow that we were leaving. However, the Lord had made it plain to us that we were to leave. We heard that P. Levi had been placed in a distant seminary - they said that he had become deranged. I didn't believe that, but felt the poor priest had problems in reconciling his convictions with the functions that were expected of him! No doubt he had displeased the authorities in Missao Velha.

Bernardo came to see us before we left. He wished to receive Jesus as his Saviour. Oh, what joy! He said he was afraid to throw his arms away - he would be dead within a few hours! We assured him that the Lord would protect him but under the circumstances we agreed that it would be better for him and his family to leave the district. It was good to be able to embrace him as a brother in Christ, knowing that we would all meet again one day!

Serafino and Alicia begged us to help them move to Juazeiro with us. Gordon went on ahead and rented a small house for us in town and another, larger one on the outskirts, in which to hold meetings. We used the large front room for meetings and Alicia and Serafino lived in the back rooms.

THIRTY-FOUR

A BRAND SNATCHED FROM THE BURNING

We soon settled our few belongings into our new house. It was in quite a good position but was very small and had a low roof. That made it get very hot.

The next task was to get to know people and give them a chance to get to know us. I met a number of young people in Juazeiro who begged us to start English classes. They were shop assistants who couldn't afford to pay very much, and so I agreed to teach them. However after a couple of lessons I was told that the priest had forbidden them to study with me. In fact, he told all the people not to talk to us! Many didn't dare to disobey the priest but a few of the braver spirits ignored his command. Ostracism is a hard thing to endure, and I felt I would rather have stone-throwing and outright aggression. However, we were soon to experience that, too!

A few poor people from the 'skid row' part of town attended our meetings - they had nothing to lose. The Lord began to work in our midst. I was glad that I had helped minister to the 'down and outs' on the Thames Embankment in London. The smells and sights I had seen there had prepared me a little for what we encountered in Juazeiro. The stuffy atmosphere in our meeting-place, where we burned little kerosene lamps, was made worse by the smell of unwashed bodies and venereal disease. We prayed for grace to endure and love to overcome the natural repugnance we felt as we ministered to these poor derelicts. Syphilis and kindred diseases were gradually destroying many of them, attacking their eyesight and finally, their brains.

One young man called Vicente began to attend our meetings

regularly. We noted his red-rimmed eyes and pock-marked skin. He listened very attentively to Gordon's preaching and on the third occasion he broke down before the Lord and accepted Him as his Saviour.

Vicente, we learned, was an alcoholic, a gambler and a frequenter of brothels. He had a wife and two children but they all had to live with his father as Vicente never had enough money to pay rent for a house of his own. He was only twenty-eight but his body was already full of disease - thin and emaciated, he looked over forty. Gordon prayed for him. That night, he went straight home to his wife and family and told them that he had become a believer and from then on would lead a different life. His father flew in a rage and ordered Vicente to take his family and get out of his house!

Shocked, they hurriedly packed their meagre belongings and left. It was ten o'clock at night and the lanes were empty. The mud huts were built in straggly rows, with a few feet of hard mud-baked earth between them, pitted with holes where mud had been made to cover the sticks stuck into the ground that formed the walls.

Slowly they made their way along the path, not knowing which direction to take. Vicente talked to his new found Father. "The missionary said that if we ask anything in the Name of Jesus, He will do it. Oh God, we need a home right now. Please find us one. In Jesus' name I ask this. Amen." Vicente's wife was crying, and the two little children, frightened by their mother's crying and the darkness of the night were crying too. They all walked on.

Suddenly they saw a woman coming toward them. "Is that you Vicente?" she cried. "Yes, it's me." he answered. "You're just the man I'm looking for," said the woman, stopping. "I've got to go to my parent's house for a few weeks and I want someone to live in my house and look after it while I'm away. Will you come? I have to leave early tomorrow morning because my mother is ill." Vicente explained his situation to the neighbour. "You'd better come back with me now then" she said. "Don't worry, there's some food in the house and you're welcome to use it. I'm glad you can stay in my place."

As in a dream, the little family accompanied their friend to her house. It was one of the better-built little houses, and in no time their hammocks had been slung up and their children put to sleep. Vicente, his wife and friend sat in the kitchen, talking over a cup of coffee. He told the friend of our meetings, and how that night he had asked Jesus to take over his life. He told of the cry that had gone up from his lips as, homeless, they had walked out of his father's house, not knowing where to go. Finally, he spoke of how, by the grace of God, he purposed to lead a new life and become a proper husband and father.

The friend listened in silence. "One of my relatives, a cousin, is a 'crente' (believer)," she said, "I have never been to one of these meetings but my cousin is a good sort and has helped my parents a lot - more than the others, who spend half their time in church, listening to the priest! If you turn out like my cousin it will be a good thing. I like you and I am glad you are going to lead a better life. Maybe I'll go to the missionary's meetings when I get back." Contentedly, they all went to their hammocks.

Vicente's wife, tired though she was, couldn't sleep for a long time, as she thought over the events of the evening. She'd grown used to her husband's ways. At least they had the security of his father's home. She'd given up hope a long time ago of ever having a place of her own. When Vicente had come home saying that he had become a 'crente' and her father-in-law had turned them out, her little world had really collapsed! Then when Vicente had asked God for a home for them, she'd begun to think that disease had started to attack his mind. Just after his prayer, Maria da Conceicao had appeared and offered them her house for an indefinite period. That was a miracle!

Did God do such things for people like them? For a man whose life had been filled with vice and whose wife had given up going to church - except for Easter, of course, when you had to go if you didn't want to lose your soul! Her mind was confused - God had never done anything for them while they were good Catholics, and yet on the very night that Vicente had 'given his heart to Jesus', He had performed a miracle. She must go with her husband to the meetings. If Vicente really changed, then life might become worth living. Hope stirred within her and she fell into a deep sleep.

THIRTY-FIVE

"HE IS ABLE TO SAVE FROM THE UTTERMOST
TO THE UTTERMOST" HEBREWS 7:25

The next morning, Vicente made his way to our home to tell us how God had performed a miracle for him - a weak, sickly layabout. Vicente felt like a worm! Now he must get a job so that he could provide properly for his family. Remorse hit him as he realized what a miserable life his wife had endured. How blind and selfish he had been!

When he got to our house he clapped his hands at the door and I invited him in. He shared the events of the previous night and we rejoiced with him, praising God. Somehow there was a different look about him already in spite of the same worn clothes and red-rimmed eyes.

We discussed his future and Gordon suddenly came up with a bright idea. He rummaged in a trunk and found a camera. It was rather old and lacking a part but it had possibilities. Vicente went off, followed by our prayers, to look for a replacement for the missing piece. He soon returned with the camera repaired, jubilant that the Lord had led him to the right place. He had bought some films and was now all set to start work.

The large market was due to be held the next day. Vicente started work early and soon ran out of film - he had so many customers! Many of his old friends came to him and he faithfully told them of what Jesus had done for him. Reactions varied. Several said that they didn't believe that Vicente could change because he was so hooked on his various vices. Others wished him well but warned him against the priest's reactions. Still others tried to turn him against the 'religion of the foreigners'.

By now the meetings took place not only in our centre but also in two mud huts on the outskirts of the 'shanty town'. We would trudge the mile and a half up the main cobbled street and then through the maze of huts to the ones where we would hold our meetings.

On our arrival we would find the little tin kerosene lamps burning smokily and a group of people sitting or standing, squashed together in the confined space. A bunch of children would be squatting on the earthen floor. These children would have often had sweet potatoes for their supper, and the resulting smells of the gases they released added to the general discomfort! We were told that the children were often sent in on purpose to do this and we were inclined to believe it!

I would start a chorus on the little piano-accordion and Gordon would try to keep them all in tune with his strong voice, as we taught the simple words. It would take them a long time to learn a hymn but, once learned, they would want it at every meeting. Gordon would then pray and preach and give the invitation to accept Jesus as their Saviour. After praying with those who responded to the appeal, we would close with another chorus.

Around this time, we would start to hear sounds from the street. The Daughters of Mary were approaching, chanting as they came. As we left the hut, stones and rubble would come flying in our direction and we would beat a hurried retreat toward home. It was always the same pattern. Sometimes we would hold an open-air meeting, and again, the rubbish lying around provided some good ammunition.

One day, a Police Sergeant who had come to listen, was hit by one of the stones by mistake. He turned around and shouted, "I'm going to become a 'crente' now. If I'm to get the stones I must get their faith!" He became a good Christian too, in spite of his unconventional conversion!

Another time, a strong character who was much respected, and rather feared, joined our ranks. Maria (no Lourdes or second name for her!) had her own special knife which was rarely far from her person. She used it to cut tough meat as well as for many other purposes. Rumor had it that it had cut into human flesh as well! A few days after she had come to the Lord, we were attacked by the usual bunch of women. Our Maria took off her wooden clog and went among them, knocking heads and whatever else got in her way! There were cries and screams as her clog found its mark. Gordon told me to run with him to her house nearby. "Get her knife," he hissed, "the daughter will know where to find it." The daughter gave it to me rather hesitantly and I took it out to Gordon, who hid it under his jacket. Sure enough, as we went back to join the mêlée, Maria came running. She went into her hut and came out shouting, "Brother Estavao, where is my knife?" Gordon calmly looked at this disheveled fury of a woman. "Maria," he said, "we don't use arms in our warfare. We let God fight for us. We must love our enemies and do good to those that persecute us, like Jesus said." The fight went right out of Maria and she dropped to her knees and sobbed, "Jesus forgive me, forgive me, I didn't know! Help me to change and have love in my heart!" After that, Maria became a true soldier for Jesus and her conduct really impressed all in her neighbourhood.

What a congregation we had! Ex-drunks, gamblers, fighters, and women of doubtful reputation. The Lord cleaned them up from inside out and made them strong and fearless witnesses to His love and grace.

THIRTY-SIX

"NO WEAPON FORMED AGAINST THEE SHALL PROSPER"
(ISA. 54:17)

One evening, a few weeks after Vicente's conversion, we met in our main meeting-place. We had advised the Colonel of Police of our meeting, as we had been instructed to do. He had told us that all of his police were busy and he wouldn't be able to keep watch over the area. Gordon told him we must hold the meeting because the people were expecting one. The Colonel retorted that we would do so at our own risk. Recognizing that pressure was being put on him by our adversaries, Gordon refused to be put off and so we went to the meeting at the appointed time.

Alicia's baby was due any day now. When we arrived at the house we found her in labour. The poor woman was lying in the back room and squatting cross-legged at the bottom of the bed was a dirty old woman with a pipe in her mouth. This was the local midwife! Alicia turned beseeching eyes to me and I could see she didn't like the idea of this woman helping her baby into the world any more than I did. Perceiving that Alicia's condition didn't seem to be presenting any complications, I decided to use my best diplomacy, and gently told the old crone that her services were no longer needed now that I had arrived, and persuaded her to leave. Alicia thanked me and we committed ourselves to the Lord and awaited developments. At Alicia's persuasion I joined the prayer meeting in the front room for a short time. There were only six people present.

A strange sound came in from the dark night - singing was coming from a large crowd, way off in the distance. Was it a holy day? We hadn't heard about it, which was unusual, as these days were usually well advertised. What were the people up to?

We were soon to learn! Vicente suggested that he do a little scouting and Gordon agreed. After a short time he returned, breathless. "There are thousands of them," he gasped. "Frei Mirocles, (the Franciscan Abbot) and his assistant, are leading them on two large horses. They are coming here and are really worked up. The people are chanting 'Long live Mary and death to the Protestants'. Brother Estevao, we will now have to prove all the things you have preached to us. Only God can save us! They have large bags of stones and rubbish to throw at us and are armed as usual. It won't stop at just throwing stones, believe me!" The men again gave themselves to prayer, interspersed with praise.

I slipped back to Alicia, who turned anxious eyes on me. Her pains were more frequent now. "What's the matter?" she whispered. Trying to treat the matter lightly, I told her that the Catholics were holding a demonstration. "Go and pray with the others," she urged. I realized that Alicia was made of sterner stuff than we had thought and did as she suggested.

From time to time, Vicente slipped out to report on the progress of the crowd. We could tell by the noise that they were getting nearer. Frei Mirocles' powerful voice could be heard. What a marvellous voice he had! It had a stirring quality about it. I realized that the man could move those crowds to do anything he wanted, and then he would just slip off and let the people get the blame for whatever happened!

Just recently, some men, members of his congregation, had been arrested by the police after giving way to their excessive zeal against us during an open-air meeting. As I had walked down the main street the day after, I had met one of them who had been imprisoned. I felt embarrassed and tried to tell the man how I regretted his arrest and that it was none of our seeking. He broke in, saying, "It is an honour to go to prison for Our Lady!" What spirit he had. How good it would be if more of us were prepared to suffer for Jesus and His Kingdom, I thought!

I was brought back sharply to reality, however, - a roar rose up from the crowd - it was so close! Vicente dashed out. Confused noises and shouts filled the air. I had to give my attention to Alicia but ran out into the front room when I heard Vicente returning.

He was excited and we could barely make sense of what he was saying. "The police have arrived and made a cordon across the road, a few yards down, just in time, because the crowd had reached the corner! The Colonel is standing in front of Frei Mirocles with his gun stuck in his belly and Mirocles is shouting at the Colonel, demanding to be allowed to pass. The Colonel is shouting back and refusing to budge!"

A police sergeant came to the open window, a broad smile on his face. "A paz do Senhor," he said. "Senhor Missionario, the Colonel wants you, please. He says you are to come and preach to that large crowd down the road!" Gordon, stunned for a moment, shouted "Praise God!" and ran out to join the sergeant. Alicia's call summoned me to her side. The baby was arriving! All my attention had to be given to the task on hand and for a while I almost forgot the drama that was taking place outside the house.

I had just finished washing the baby and Alicia when there was a noise outside the room. I looked up to see the sergeant with two policemen standing in the doorway. "Sister, your husband has just finished preaching to Frei Mirocles' congregation and so we are escorting him home. Two of my men will take you home when you are ready. God has done a wonderful thing tonight. All is well!" The Sergeant and his men then left.

Some believers came to see us, laughing and praising God, and we asked them what had happened. They told us that Frei Mirocles was so disgusted with the Colonel that he finally called him a 'dirty Protestant'! That proved too much for the poor Colonel, who promptly sent the sergeant to fetch Gordon down to preach to the multitude. Mirocles and his companion, on horseback, had wheeled around and thundered off down the cobbled road, leaving the mob, confused, standing there. Gordon had then appeared and immediately taken advantage of the situation, God giving him wisdom to preach His love to those poor misguided people. He had a strong voice, and standing on a low wall, his words carried down the hill to those crowds still pressing forward.

After a few minutes, realizing that the tables had been turned, some of the leaders urged the people to go home. Many were reluctant to do so, however, and pushed their way forward in order to hear the foreigner more clearly. Certain elements among the crowd got angry, however, and started rousing the people against Gordon once more, so the Colonel asked him to stop. Many had heard and seen much to make them think, though, and the events of that night provided the theme of all conversations in town for several days afterwards. Frei Mirocles had 'lost face' and his people saw that the other foreigners had the backing of the law. The Italian Abbot had been made to realize that he could no longer flout Brazilian law with impunity. He would have to change his tactics and change them he did! He couldn't touch the other foreigners and so he would try to eliminate their followers!

A little later, leaving a tired but happy Alicia with Serafino and their new baby, I was duly escorted home by the two policemen. Gordon and I were tired but too excited to sleep. How did a Christian Police sergeant manage to turn up in Juazeiro last night of all nights? We finally dropped off to sleep.

The next morning we received a visit from a beaming Sgt. Miguel. As we sat down to have coffee together, we waited eagerly for his account of how he came to Juazeiro.

It appeared that Bro. Teixeira's church had been much in prayer for us. We hadn't written to them since we had arrived in Juazeiro, but knowing the city's reputation, Bro. Teixeira knew we would encounter stiff opposition. Bro. Miguel, who was a member of the church, felt strongly impressed to ask for a transfer into the interior, which was granted. He and his wife had moved to Juazeiro just a couple of days ago. While familiarizing himself with the layout of the city and fulfilling his duties, he had heard rumours of what was being planned against us. Being an intelligent and wise man, he succeeded in verifying the rumours. By this time, night had fallen, but he went straight to the Colonel with his information.

At first the Colonel lightly dismissed Miguel's report of the planned attack, and said it was none of his affair. At that, Miguel said the Holy Spirit came upon him powerfully, and, pointing his finger at the Colonel, he said, "The blood of the missionaries will be on your head, Colonel!" The officer shook, sat up abruptly and started giving orders to his men.

He and twenty policemen arrived just as Frei Mirocles and his crowd had reached the corner of the road, barely twenty yards from our meeting-place!

How we praised God together! To us, the attack of the previous night had come as an unpleasant surprise, but the Lord had known in advance of the evil thoughts of our enemies and made provision for our protection, putting it in the heart of Miguel to ask for a transfer. The situation did not take the Lord by surprise! There is a scripture of which I am very fond, Eph. 2:10, which says, "For we are God's workmanship, created in Christ Jesus to do good works, which God prepared in advance for us to do." As we follow the guidance of the Holy Spirit, we can be sure that help and provision will be forthcoming all along the way! The angel of the Lord will be there to avert disaster or to see that needs are supplied. How wonderful are His ways! The Holy Spirit motivates us to follow the Lord's plan while His angels are there to minister to us as we obey Him!

Sergeant Miguel didn't remain very long in Juazeiro. He was transferred back to Fortaleza after a few weeks.

THIRTY-SEVEN

GOD'S WORD AGAIN PUT TO THE TEST

Vicente's fearless testimony drew the attention of our adversaries to him. One day he saw four armed men approaching his house and knew instinctively that they meant him harm. He called to his wife, took his children and they all slipped out of the back yard and came down to me. Gordon was away on his preaching circuit at that time, so we prayed, seeking to know how to deal with the situation. Afterwards I felt I should report the matter to the police, so Vicente and I went straight to the Colonel, telling the family to follow us.

After explaining the situation to the Colonel, he asked me, "Did those men come to attack you?" "No," I replied, "but this man is my brother, and what is done against him is done against me. He is my brother because he has given his life to the Lord Jesus Christ." The Colonel was startled, looking at Vicente's swarthy countenance. "Your brother, senhora? But he is a Brazilian! What does the Lord have to do with it!" The Colonel could see that he was dealing with an unreasonable woman. "I will take care of the matter, senhora," he said soothingly. "You can go home now and leave the matter to me."

The attitude of the Colonel upset me. His orders were only to protect the foreign Protestants and it didn't matter what was done to poor Brazilian peasants. An hitherto unknown feeling of strong anger possessed me! "Colonel, I want you to provide Vicente with two soldiers to escort him and his family home. The soldiers must remain on guard for at least two hours, so that the people in the area will know that the Brazilian government protects its citizens!" Cold fury lent an edge to my words and the Colonel dropped his eyes. "I will wait until you have issued the order!" I said.

The Colonel realized that he wouldn't get rid of me until he had acceded to my demand. He sighed and gave the order to the soldier standing by. The matter would get round the barracks and the men would enjoy a huge joke at his expense, he thought ruefully! He gave orders to two soldiers who had arrived. Surely the English woman would go now!

I had a feeling that the Colonel would cancel the order when I'd gone, so I stood there, waiting for the soldiers to move out with Vicente and his family, who had just arrived. The Colonel got exasperated. "You can go now, senhora" he said. "The matter is dealt with." "I am waiting to see the soldiers take the family home," I replied. The Colonel curtly ordered the soldiers to move out. I went to the gate and watched the group until they had reached the top of the main street and moved out of sight. I felt tired - all the fight had gone out of me. Another battle won, I thought, but what would happen next? It seemed one long struggle, with everything against us. I remembered a line from an old wartime song, "There's no discharge in the war!" Then another line came to mind, from the Bible, "If God is for us, who can be against us?" Romans 8:31. Peace returned to my heart.

As I walked slowly home, I thought about my strange life. For two half-days a week I taught English in Crato, visiting homes where I was treated with respect and even affection, by my students, who were growing in number. I had several classes and individual students, all over the city, besides the one in Snr. Neri's home. After class, my pupils would talk with me and I often had meals with them. I loved the hours spent away from Juazeiro, with all its fanaticism and hate. Meeting with the educated Brazilians made a welcome respite from the squalor and ignorance we met with on the outskirts of Juazeiro.

THIRTY-EIGHT

"GOD CHOOSES THE WEAK THINGS TO CONFOUND THE MIGHTY" I CORINTHIANS 1:27

The aborted attempt on Vicente's life had really upset Gordon and me. We wondered what Mirocles would do next. That he was behind it, we had no doubt whatever - the Brazilians said so. One morning we had our usual time of prayer after breakfast and sat discussing the situation. "Why don't you go and see Mirocles, Gordon, and make him realize the seriousness of what he is doing?" I said. "It's no good Jackie, they wouldn't even let me in the monastery," he said. "Don (a Baptist missionary friend) tried it once without success." "Then let me go. Maybe they'll let a woman in!" I suggested. "I don't see that you can do much good by going, but you can try if you like," Gordon replied.

I put on my shoes and left immediately, knowing that when he had time to think about it, Gordon would change his mind! A few minutes' brisk walk brought me to the large, imposing gate of the Franciscan monastery. I pulled the big iron bell-handle and the clang of the bell sounded harshly through the courtyard. As the sound faded, I suddenly realized what I was doing. Here was I, a non-Catholic woman, seeking audience with a renowned Protestant-hater. Once more I was in the lion's den! 'Fools step in where angels fear to tread'. That just about described me!

A tall young Franciscan came to the gate. "What do you want?" he asked. "I want to speak to Frei Mirocles, please." I answered. The monk looked at me curiously. "You are the English missionary's wife, are you not?" he asked. I admitted that I was, and my hopes fell sharply. "Please wait a minute," he said.

How those minutes dragged by! I tried to concentrate on thinking about what I was going to say to the Abbot but I couldn't decide on the best approach. The ludicrousness of the situation was borne upon me and my knees felt like jelly. "You've taken too much upon yourself this time, my girl," I told myself. Then I thought maybe this was a leading of the Holy Spirit after all. Hadn't we prayed that morning, just before the idea came to me of visiting the Abbot? Didn't God use the weak things of this world to confound the mighty and foolish things to shame the wise? (1 Cor. 1:27). I certainly qualified! Then I also remembered the Scripture in Luke 21:15, "For I will give you words of wisdom that none of your adversaries will be able to resist or contradict." I sent up an SOS to the Lord, " Please fulfill your promise to me now, Lord!"

The Franciscan came and opened the gate. "Please come in," he said. The big iron gate clanged shut behind me, and we entered the main building. I was led down some rather dark passages and then up some stairs, stopping before a large, imposing door. The young monk knocked, rather timidly, and Frei Mirocles' voice boomed out, "Come in." The monk opened the door, ushered me in and then left.

I found myself face to face with a large, stout man, dressed in the brown habit of the Franciscans, with a white girdle around his ample waist. His round, fat face was heavily bearded with full, red sensuous lips and red-rimmed 'piggy' eyes. Those eyes glared at me and I shuddered at the hate in them. I seemed to be looking at Satan himself, so malevolent and threatening was the whole appearance of this man! My mouth felt dry.

"Why have they sent a woman to me?" he shouted. I replied firmly, "God sent me, Frei Mirocles." "You have courage to come here," he countered. "I fear God, not man," I replied.

The Abbot paced the room, his hands clasped behind his back. "Sit down," he ordered, indicating a chair by his desk. My legs had almost been giving way, so I sat down with alacrity! The Abbot stopped and faced me. "You people are preparing the way for the Communists!" he accused. This absurd statement surprised me. "Senhor how can you say that? The Communists have gained more power in Italy than in any other part of Europe, and have done so in spite of the presence of the Vatican." This was true at that time. The Abbot sat down. I think that he was surprised that I should be so knowledgeable. "Well, tell me why you've come here," he barked. I told him quietly but firmly, that we objected to his attacks on the simple Brazilians who came to our meetings. We were prepared to put up with personal persecution because we were called by God to preach the Gospel, but he, as a foreigner, should permit the natives of the land to choose their own religion. As a fellow-guest in Brazil, he should not endanger the lives of the nationals or encourage them to break their own laws. He strongly denied knowledge of these attacks and blamed the Brazilians but I told him that people had told us that he was the instigator of them.

I could see that the Abbot was shaken. In that gross hulk of a body was a mean, cowardly soul and I felt the Spirit of God rising within me. "These people are liars and killers," he said, "you can't believe what they say!"

A thought came to me like a flash from heaven! "How long have you been here?" I asked. He drew himself up. "Seventeen years," he said. "My, what have you been preaching all that time?" I asked in a quiet voice. "Our experience is that, when the people hear and accept the Gospel of Jesus, they change. They no longer lie and kill but become honest citizens and loving people!"

I pursued my theme, pointing out the teachings of Jesus as the Holy spirit directed me. I was filled with compassion for the man and felt the love of God clothing my words.

The Abbot didn't look at me but sat, fingering his beard nervously. Suddenly there was a knock on the door and the young Franciscan announced the arrival of two Brazilian priests. The attitude of the Abbot changed. He got up abruptly and thanked me for my visit. "I will consider what you have said, but, of course, we will continue to oppose you." I reminded him quietly that he was not opposing us but the truth of God. He again glared at me but there was something different about that glare. It had lost some of its arrogance and hate. I looked him straight in the eyes and told him that we were praying for him. He stuttered, "Goodbye," and I was ushered out as the two Brazilians came in, looking at me curiously.

When I arrived home I collapsed into my hammock and Gordon made me a cup of tea. "How did it go?" he asked eagerly. "Give me a few minutes to recover," I begged. Once again I had proved the power of God to take over a weak vessel to accomplish His purposes but afterwards, as usual, I was made to feel my weakness! 'We have this treasure in earthen vessels, that the surpassing greatness of the power may be of God and not from ourselves.'- 2 Cor. 4:7.

THIRTY-NINE

"MY GRACE IS SUFFICIENT FOR YOU..." II CORINTHIANS 12:9

Life went on as usual. I spent two days in Crato, teaching, and we held meetings in Juazeiro and surrounding villages. Many came to know Jesus and the congregations grew. We noted that no more attacks were made on the lives of the believers and we praised God.

Our little house was like an oven. It was composed of three small rooms and a lean-to kitchen, with the usual toilet and shower in the hut in the small back yard. In our front room we had three canvas-seated chairs, a small table and simple bookcase. In the bedroom there was only room for two pallet beds with grass mattresses and a wooden trunk for our clothes. A rod was fixed on the wall on which to hang our few suits and dresses. A simple wooden table and four chairs in the 'dining-room', a primitive wood-burning stove and two large water pots, with three shelves on the wall in the kitchen, completed the furnishings. In the hottest months we slept in hammocks. The floors were of cement and there were no ceilings, just rafters with clay tiles above. We had no fan and the heat was stifling! Neither did we have a radio. I must admit that I yearned, sometimes, for a few home comforts!

One day a poor woman came to the house, asking if she could do our washing to earn some money. I soon made up a bundle of clothes and handed them over to her with the customary bar of soap. That was the last I saw of her or of the clothes!

One morning, I noted two tiny specks of blood on the upper part of my chest. They were like little pin pricks, and the next day there were more. I couldn't think what they might be. We had just bought new grass-filled mattresses, so they couldn't be caused from the tiny bugs that habitually hatch out in the grass over a period of a few weeks, aided by the warmth from our bodies. That night, Gordon awoke and turned his flashlight on. He let out an exclamation as he directed the beam on to the rafters above my bed. The light disturbed the two objects hanging just above my body. Gordon flung the wooden shutters open and somehow got the 'objects' out. They were small vampire bats!

FORTY

GREAT EXPECTATIONS

Excitement filled the air! Our Lady of Fatima, a small jewel-encrusted statue of the Virgin Mary had been brought from Portugal to Brazil. She was accredited with miraculous powers and she, with her retinue of priests, were making a tour throughout the country, visiting all the major towns and cities. Rumours spread daily of miracles performed in this or that place, and preparations were made for her to come to this half-forgotten area of the Northeast. A special carriage would bring her from the coast by train, and she would spend a few hours in the larger towns enroute to Crato, the end of the railway line. Juazeiro was on the itinerary, and expectations ran high as the day of her anticipated arrival drew near.

One day, on my usual visit to Crato, I greeted P. Montenegro on his arrival at our class. This usually calm and dignified man was obviously agitated. On my asking what the matter was, he sat on the chair and remarked that I would never believe what he was about to tell me!

The itinerary of the statue had been changed. The officials in Juazeiro had been advised that it would not stop there, after all. An uproar had ensued as this news became public and finally a committee had been formed and word sent to Crato, that, if the original program was not adhered to, the people of Juazeiro would rise up and kill the Bishop! "Impossible! I cried" Oh no, not in this part of the country!" said the priest.

"Some twenty years ago the government had to send planes to drop a couple of bombs on the outskirts of Juazeiro, because its fanaticism had led the people into forming a so-called 'holy city' where sacrilegious acts were being committed in the name of religion. Certain individuals took the names of the Holy Family and saints and the people refused to submit to the laws of the land. The threat to kill the Bishop cannot be taken lightly!"

The next day I went to the private nursing home of one of my doctor pupils, to give him his lesson. He looked grim. Dr. Gesteira was a fine-looking man in his forties, and was recognized as one of the best surgeons in the region. He received medical journals in English, French and German, regularly. The learning of these professional men in the interior of Brazil never ceased to amaze me! Dr. Gesteira was much involved in politics and well-known for his kindness to the poor.

My doctor friend talked to me about the situation in Juazeiro. He explained that the Colonel of Police there was an acquaintance of his and came over once a week to inform him of our activities in the area and the reactions of the people. He told us that the Colonel had told him of the planned attack against Vicente and then asked me what actually happened. How he laughed when I told him of the discomfiture of the Colonel at my insistence on his protection of Vicente! Dr. Gesteira told me that the Colonel reckoned that I was a 'strong woman' and the Doctor shouldn't worry about my well-being! We had a good laugh together and then the doctor became serious. He said that the situation in Juazeiro was grave, as the visit of Fatima was raising religious fervour to fever-pitch. He told me that we must not hold any meetings during her visit. I explained that the visit of Fatima coincided with the monthly visits that Gordon made to the outlying villages, and that I would therefore be alone at that time.

Dr. Gesteira was upset when he heard this and asked me to come over to Crato and stay at his nursing-home, 'where they could look after me'. I was touched by his concern and thanked him but had to refuse his kind offer. How could I leave our little flock at a time like this? My friend gazed at me, worriedly, but said no more, other than warning me not to leave the house during the visit of the statue. I knew that the Colonel would be receiving a strict admonition to see that no harm came to me!

I had one more day of classes in Crato before the statue was due to arrive. In the evening, I taught at the house of a young bank clerk. His family was always very kind to me and I sometimes had supper with them after the lesson. On this occasion, I was introduced to the elder brother, who was a priest. The young man looked pale and had two days' growth of beard. His eyes were red-rimmed with tiredness, and he told me that he had been in church, hearing confessions non-stop for two days, with just a couple of hours' sleep. Such was the desire of people to get right with God before the arrival of Fatima.

I returned to Juazeiro. The coming of Fatima was the only topic of conversation. I heard young servant-girls saying that they were giving their jewellry to her. Poor women who could barely feed their large families were going without their main meal for two or three days, so as to save a few cruzeiros to give to the statue. Others spoke of the surrounding villages bringing in their sick for her to heal. My heart sank lower and lower - I didn't believe the stories we had heard about the miraculous cures and I felt sad that these poor people were having their hopes raised only to be disappointed and disillusioned. Accounts of the money raised for the image also got spread around. Her coffers were overflowing with costly jewellry and millions of cruzeiros. How could they take the money of the poor like this - from people who counted themselves happy if they had one meal a day of beans and rice, with a bit of meat occasionally to go with it?

FORTY-ONE

"YOU SHALL NOT BOW DOWN YOURSELVES TO THEM"
EXODUS 32:24

The great day arrived! People poured into town. Some were pushing carts with sick people in them. Others came in on mules and on the backs of lorries. Many carried their sick and crippled loved-ones on their shoulders. Ignoring the doctor's admonition to stay home, I went out to the main street and watched this tide of humanity sweeping into the town. Crowds surrounded the railway station where Fatima was due to arrive that afternoon. A Mass was to be held in the evening in the large central church and a procession was to be formed to go through the town with the statue the next morning.

I went home for a meal but left the house again in the early evening when it was dark. As if drawn by a magnet, I went near the church and saw the light of hundreds of candles burning. People who could not get in filled the square outside, and the great door of the church was left open. I couldn't get near enough to see inside but chanting filled the air. Deeply depressed, I went home to bed, after praying for the people. How my heart ached for them!

The next morning I was up early. Knowing that the procession was due to pass the end of our street, I couldn't resist the impulse to join the crowds at the corner awaiting the procession. People jammed the pavement and I was pushed near the curb, completely hemmed in. Then the procession came into view. First came the Daughters, and then the Sons of Mary, flanked by the Franciscan monks and priests from the area, followed by a highly-polished limousine, on which stood the four-foot high image of Fatima. She was decked in a golden crown and jewels with satin streamers flowing from her over the silks and brocades which decorated the top of the car. More priests and dignitaries of the town followed behind.

As the procession came slowly up the main street, the people dropped to their knees and a hush came over the crowds. I felt hot and cold alternately. What was I to do? I couldn't move because of the press of the crowd around me and it would cause a disturbance if I tried to push my way out. I must just stay put and trust the Lord to keep me safe. Sweat poured from me as the procession drew level with us. All around me people were sinking to their knees. Those on my side of the procession looked at me. I gazed at them steadily, especially at one German priest, whom I had met and spoken to in Crato. He lowered his eyes as they encountered mine.

The procession passed up the street and the people around gradually got up. Hostile looks were directed at me but I gently pushed my way out of the crowd and went home. The scenes I had witnessed were printed indelibly on my mind. At no time has the sin of idolatry come home to me as it did then! As I thought about these people whose lives were so hard, so hopeless in their poverty and sickness, so fear-ridden until the day they died, my heart was again filled with compassion. Gordon and I would continue to give them the liberating Gospel, at whatever cost!

In the afternoon I slipped out again, this time to watch the disappointed multitudes winding their weary way home. The sick were still in the carts or on the backs of relatives. No mighty miracles had been performed. Not one person had been healed at the magnificent mass, held in all the pomp and glitter that previous night. Their pockets lighter, but hearts that were heavier, the young, old and infirm struggled up the cobbled street. Silently the crowds dispersed and faced their daily tasks once again. What were their thoughts, I wondered? Did some of them harbour doubts about their religion? These could never be put into words, of course, they were sinful and must not be uttered. Surely their church, their learned priests and monks could not be wrong? The fault must be with them

- they were too poor and ignorant for the blessed holy Virgin of Fatima to do anything for them! They must do more penance, perhaps. This suffering must be the will of God for them. I learned about some of these thoughts later on, from some of the dear folks who came to our meetings.

FORTY-TWO

"INSTANT IN SEASON, OUT OF SEASON" II TIMOTHY 4:2

A couple of weeks later, P. Montenegro told me that he could no longer study with me as he had been made Chaplain of the Hospital and these extra duties would leave him with no time to attend class. After the lesson he quietly asked me if I would teach him privately, in his office. Of course I agreed, but noticed that Snr. Neri was watching me like a hawk. I wasn't sure whether he had heard our conversation or not. Anyway, the next week, on the morning following our usual evening class, I went to the priest's office at the college. Sadly he informed me that he would not be able to continue his study with me, after all. As I shook hands with him on leaving, he said quietly, "Please look upon me as your friend. If you ever need any help, come to me."

I knew why he couldn't study with me - pressure had been put on him by his superiors. I thanked God that I had been able to put the Bible way of salvation so clearly to him during our talks.

My journeys to and from Crato were made in a rickety old bus. Women with all sorts of merchandise would crowd on and more than once I'd had chickens under my seat and had to watch they didn't peck my bare legs!

I didn't think that my pupils knew of our poverty until one day, one of them, a businessman, suddenly asked me, "Dona Jacquelina, why does your mission send you here to starve?" I looked at him, startled. Gordon and I had asked the Lord, "Why?" on several occasions, ourselves. I sent up an SOS to Him. The answer came, swiftly.

After telling Snr. Paulo that we had not been sent by a Mission but by the Lord, I then explained that we were working among people who lived on the verge of starvation and who often did not know where their next meal was coming from. In order to help them, I continued, we must live under similar conditions and prove God in their midst. As we found His promises to be true in every situation, then we could encourage them to look to Him for help in their lives too. They would know that they could believe His Word because our lives were open for them to see how He supplied our needs. We were his showpieces - Ephesians 2:10.

I knew that Snr. Paulo was going through a difficult time himself. His wife, also my pupil, had held a good job and had recently given birth to twins. As a result she had given up working. The long drought had affected their business and, accustomed as they were to a high standard of living, they were finding it difficult to make ends meet. I told Snr. Paulo about several occasions when the Lord had answered prayer for personal needs, and explained what the Bible said about God taking care of us, if we committed our lives wholly to Him. I could speak more freely with him than with his wife, who was a practicing Catholic. As was often the case in the various homes that I visited, one member of the family would be willing to discuss spiritual matters when alone with me, while the others were obviously afraid and exerted pressure on them. However, I prayed that one day the Lord would move in the area and make it possible for those dear people to break loose from the system by which they were bound.

Not long after this, I woke up one morning, feeling really ill. My head was bad and I had stomach pains and a fever. I was due to go to Crato to teach but that was out of the question, feeling as I did. Gordon phoned from the Post Office to tell some of my students including Dr. Gesteira.

Forty-five minutes later, the doctor arrived by car. He gave me a quick examination and then turned to Gordon. "It's para-typhoid and I must take her back with me. Don't worry, she will have the best of care in my nursing-home."

I remember little of what happened during the next few days, but, as I began to feel better, I was able to enjoy the care and good food that I was receiving. Fish was brought in by train once a week for the rich people's Club and some was procured for me. It was two years or more since I'd had fresh fish. What a luxury! My bed was in the best room of the nursing-home. How good it was to stretch out on the comfortable mattress!

Among my visitors was the German priest, who was there to see one of his parishioners. After a little general conversation, we got on to the matter of religion. I spoke to him about the 'rapture' - the coming of Jesus for His people before the wrath of God is poured out upon the earth. Father Frederico was completely ignorant of the prophecies concerning this event, and the later return of Jesus to set up His Kingdom on the earth. He listened with interest as I gave him some references from the Bible, and was very thoughtful as he left me. I felt it was worthwhile having para-typhoid to have the opportunity of talking to this man!

FORTY-THREE

A WELCOME BREAK

When I was well enough, the doctor arranged for my transfer to a small hotel in the town, which was owned by the parents of another of my pupils, where I could recuperate while still under his watchful eyes. He wouldn't take any payment from us! How wonderfully the Lord provides for those who put their whole trust in Him. The doctor suggested that I should go to the coast for a while, so Gordon arranged for me to go to Pastor Teixeira's home in Fortaleza for a few days. He couldn't afford to accompany me on the bus but decided he would try to get a lift in a lorry, later.

On the day before I was due to leave for Fortaleza, I went out for a walk to visit a pupil. I met P. Montenegro and he stopped to asked me how I was feeling. When I told him I was still rather weak but was going to the coast to recuperate, he asked me how I was travelling. I told him that I was getting the bus the next morning. A smile lit up his face - "One of my priests, P. Mario, is going on that bus. I will tell him to look after you!" Noting my look of dismay, he laughed outright. "But P. Mario hates Protestants and he also hates women!" I protested. "It will do him good," retorted my friend and wishing me a speedy return to health he bowed and left me.

The next morning sure enough, P. Mario introduced himself at the bus stop. He was obviously embarrassed and straight away ushered me into a seat right at the back of the bus. Then he turned and took a seat right in the front! As we started off, I asked the Lord to give me a seat next to the priest. After about an hour, the man sitting next to P. Mario got off the bus. I slipped down to the front and took his place! Knowing the priest to be a very clever man and a historian, I started to ask him about the places we were passing through and that broke the ice. From then on I was given a very interesting account of the background of that large area.

When entering one town, P. Mario told me that they had once had an invasion by monks. He was speaking in English, and although I admired his grasp of the language, somehow I felt that he had made a mistake. I pressed for more details in order to find out what he was trying to say, not daring to say that he might be using the wrong word - he was a fiercely proud little man. As it dawned on me that the word he should have used was 'monkeys', I had difficulty in not laughing out loud! Carefully, I tried to tell him the difference between the two words, so small and yet so significant, but he got huffy and so I changed the subject. The rest of the journey passed pleasantly, apart from the heat and roughness of the road, and we arrived in Fortaleza in the evening. P. Mario waited with me until a lady from the church came to fetch me, and then he bowed stiffly and went on his way.

The ten days on the coast did me a lot of good. Gordon joined me later and took me to visit the British Consul and his wife, who made us very welcome. The Consul was the son of a Presbyterian Pastor and they had lived in Southern Ireland for a number of years. He therefore understood the problems we were up against in the interior.

I also enjoyed staying with Pastor Teixeira and his wife, Francesca. They appreciated the fact that we, foreigners, were willing to go into the difficult places with the Gospel, thus making a way for the Brazilians to follow on at a later date.

FORTY-FOUR

A HAPPY EVENT

The time came for us to return to Juazeiro. Leaving the beautiful, unspoiled coast and our kind friends was difficult. How we had enjoyed the worship in the church services, free from harassment and attack! I began to appreciate a little of what it meant for Jesus to 'set his face as a flint', as he returned to Jerusalem to meet his enemies!

In spite of the attempts of my pupils to be friendly, there was always this barrier between us - this fear on their part to talk about the Gospel. One young lad in his early teens, who later came to our house to study with me, would burst out with a question about Jesus, the Virgin Mary or some doctrine, from time to time, but always begged me not to tell anybody that he had discussed religion with me. His parents had told him that they would whip him if he did. During the short break in our lesson, I told him all I could about the Gospel, and believe that he came to trust Jesus as his Saviour before he stopped coming to see me. It was a sad situation. One young convert in Juazeiro, a lad of about fourteen, came regularly to the meetings. He asked for prayer for his parents who regularly beat him on his return home. Thank God, he never stopped coming.

One day, about three months after our return to Juazeiro I realized I was going to have another child and Dr. Gesteira confirmed it. After our usual class, he turned to me and said seriously, "Dona Jacquelina, now you are expecting a child, you can't live any longer in Juazeiro. You must come to Crato to live, where we can take care of you. The Colonel keeps me informed of the situation in Juazeiro and I know it's still not good. For the sake of your baby you must leave. Please tell your husband what I've said."

When I told Gordon that a little one was definitely on the way and that the doctor had advised a move to Crato, he agreed that we should go. He could still visit Juazeiro and the other congregations from a base in Crato.

It was a relief to leave that little oven of a house in the city, where the powers of darkness were so strong. Even two unbelieving foreigners, passing through one day and meeting Gordon in a cafe, remarked to him about the strange atmosphere in the place, and said they would be glad to leave!

We found a roomy, farmhouse style place to live in, just on the borders of Crato. It had a garden and there was a peaceful air about it. We bought a little more simple second-hand furniture and settled down to await the birth of the baby. Surely our guardian angels had gone before us to prepare this place! We knew that no one would be able to harm us there, because through my teaching, I had made friends with some of the most influential people in the city. The Lord had surely closed the mouth of the lions!

My pupils were delighted, of course. I was able to relax for the first time in many months, and my health improved. Gordon enthusiastically started working on the garden in the cooler hours of the day, much to the amazement of the Brazilians, who do not put their hands to such menial tasks as digging, etc.! Only the poorest peasant does such work. However, the Lord blessed his labours and we benefited greatly from the produce. Our tomatoes were the envy of the district!

Transport was always one of the biggest problems. Gordon needed to get around the surrounding villages and scattered farms. One of my pupils had some horses and he agreed to lend one to Gordon for this purpose, when he had no other way of travelling.

It was agreed that I should notify him a few days ahead, before the animal was needed, so that he could feed the horse well before it carried Gordon! The German priest, P. Frederico, who was half as large again as Gordon, had the same problem over transport and my pupil agreed to rent him a horse as well. However, when the priest lifted his massive frame on to the poor animal, it just sat down. P. Frederico, having more money than we had, bought himself a motorbike! It was a joke among the Brazilians that 'Fred-é-rico' means 'Fred is rich'!

What a contrast to my grass mattress in the front bedroom in Patos! Here I was, again in the best room in Dr. Gesteira's nursing-home. This time I had the luxury of a fan during my labour. All went well and Malcolm came into the world just as the midwife arrived. The doctor came later, looked at Malcolm's feet and commented that he was going to be tall! Another doctor, also my pupil, took us home in his jeep when we left the nursing-home. How we thanked God for all of His goodness.

FORTY-FIVE

"COMMIT YOUR WAY UNTO THE LORD..." PSALM 37:5

One day, a beggar knocked at our door and Gordon opened it to be confronted by a long snake dangling from the beggar's stick. It was dead and the beggar explained that he had just killed it as it was entering our house through a small hole in the wall! Gordon gratefully gave him a generous reward, and the man and the snake moved on down the road. A little later, Gordon went into town and passed the beggar, going through the same performance outside the door of another house, with the same snake! How we laughed at our own gullibility.

Unhappily, after a few months we had to leave the house, as the owner wanted to occupy it himself. We therefore moved into the town, which was more convenient for my teaching.

Strangely enough, our congregation on the outskirts of town never grew very big. Only the poorest, who had nothing to lose, came. There was no persecution but no growth either. Being the seat of the Bishop and the place where the Catholic Action newspaper was printed, as well as being filled with Seminaries and Colleges, most people did not dare to attend our meetings. Priests and nuns abounded in the streets and the business premises. Processions, accompanied by fervent singing, paraded through the city at night on the frequent holy days. The city seemed bent on impressing all with its religious zeal!

I discovered that in many of the families I visited, the eldest son or daughter was a priest or nun. In fact many of the families would sacrifice to give the eldest children an education that would enable them to qualify for this position.

The rains came, mercifully, after a five-year drought. They were heavy and I had to put bowls in the kitchen and living-room to catch the water that came through the broken tiles on the roof. I put a large umbrella over us in bed. Everything seemed damp. Malcolm who was now ten months old, caught pneumonia but with the aid of our doctor friend, I nursed him back to health. However, feeding him until then had depleted my health and the doctor said that we should both go back to England for a furlough. It was almost six years since we had left England and the rigors of our life had taken their toll on my never very robust frame. We sought the Lord for money to pay our fares, and within three months enough had come in for Malcolm and I. Gordon decided that we should go on ahead and that he would follow as soon as he had enough for his fare.

FORTY-SIX

TIME FOR A FURLOUGH

The Lord arranged our trip to the coast by sending an English businessman to Crato whom we met 'by chance'. He volunteered to escort Malcolm and myself to our friends on the coast, who would see us aboard the boat. Reluctant to leave Gordon, I nevertheless accepted this provision of the Lord and with Malcolm in my arms, I boarded the ancient aeroplane that was to take us to the coast. This rickety machine somehow made it to Fortaleza, where we spent the night with the businessman's family. From there we were taken to the boat and found ourselves enroute to England.

After a pleasant journey, with delicious food, we finally arrived in Southampton. Friends waiting there passed me by at first. Suddenly they turned back and looking hard at me, they ran up excitedly and hugged Malcolm and myself. "Oh Jackie, how thin you are - we just didn't recognize you!" they said. We were taken home to see some dear friends, Mr. and Mrs. Parnell, while waiting for Gordon to join us. Later we were told that I had looked as though I had just come out of a concentration camp!

Gordon worked on faithfully while waiting for his fare to come in. Finally, after six months, he felt he should pack and store our few belongings and travel up to Bélem. There at an English Bank, he saw the Manager and asked if he could take a loan to complete his passage money to England. The Manager was kind but said that he couldn't help. Gordon's hopes fell. He had felt so sure of the Lord's leading! As he sadly left the Manager's office, a young clerk called to him. He and another clerk explained to Gordon that they had heard him talking to the Manager. They went on to say they would lend him the money!

Joyfully, Gordon went to the shipping company to book his passage. The clerk explained regretfully that there was no vacancy on the boat due to sail the next day. It would be weeks before another boat was due. Gordon gave the clerk the phone number of the place where he was staying and asked him to ring if there should be a cancellation. He went back to his room to pray. At peace, he had a good night's sleep. The next morning the receptionist called him to the phone. The clerk's voice informed him that a cancellation had just been made and that if he went down straight away, they could arrange a berth for him! How gracious the Lord is to His children! The Scripture says, "For as many are led by the Spirit of God, they are the sons of God." Gordon truly felt the son of a King when he pondered over what the Lord had done in his situation!

FORTY-SEVEN

A COUPLE OF JONAHS?

By the time that Gordon arrived in England, the rest of the money had come in for the fare, and he was able to pay back the loan made by the kind young clerks. My health was much improved and after a short stay in Devonshire, we commenced our itinerary. The Lord blessed our ministry and we were much encouraged by the good numbers of believers who pledged us their support.

The beginning of 1957 found us preparing for our return to Brazil. Various factors caused us to decide to form our own Mission. An old friend of Gordon's, Mr. Edgar Parnell, became our Secretary and dealt with our affairs in England. His business acumen was a real blessing to us. He and his dear wife, Doris, were true friends who always warmly welcomed us into their home and made us feel part of the family.

Seeking a cheap passage for us, Gordon heard of a boat leaving Liverpool in early February - not the best of times to cross the Atlantic! It was a 14,000 ton, flat-bottomed vessel that was being taken over to be used on the River Amazon. When we embarked, we found that there was only one other passenger besides ourselves, who was going to Ecuador. There was no stewardess and I was to be the only woman on board.

After the first few days I became seasick and had to remain in my bunk. We ran into really bad weather and even Gordon, normally a good sailor, was seasick for twenty-four hours. The only one on board who didn't suffer was Malcolm, now two years old!

For eight days I remained in our berth and when I finally managed to stagger out of our cabin, I found him down in the galley, watching the cook peel potatoes! I learned that the crew had taken turns in looking after our son! After a couple of days' respite we ran into another tempest and I was again confined to my berth. I tried to remain on deck, as Gordon did, but was advised to go below. The sea rose up like mountains before and behind us and our small boat seemed so frail as we plunged into the valleys between the high waves. Everybody was seasick!

In all, we went through seven tempests. The sea broke through the dining-saloon portholes and crashed across the room, breaking the glass in the cabinet on the other side. Everything broke loose down in the hold! When I managed to get a meal in an interlude between storms, the Chief Engineer came to us and asked, quite seriously, "You are not a couple of Jonahs by any chance, are you?" We were able to reassure him on this point and affirmed that whatever happened on the voyage, we would certainly reach our destination, as we were doing the will of God. He passed this information round the boat and I think it heartened the crew, as several remarks were made that showed us that morale was improving!

What a voyage! It took us three weeks, instead of two to reach Brazil. The Captain told us that he would never take a flat-bottomed boat across the Atlantic again, especially in February! Amazingly, in spite of the damage done to much of the stuff in the hold, our packing-cases were intact, except for one corner which was broken. The shipping company replaced the article that became slightly damaged as a result.

FORTY-EIGHT

"THE LORD CONFIRMS HIS WORD" MARK 16:20

Somewhat shaky after our harrowing experiences, we arrived back in Brazil and made our way to a town in Minas Gerais. We had been advised not to return to the Northeast because of my health. While spending a day in Belo Horizonte, the State capital, we met one of my pupils from Crato, Dr. Thadeus, who was down for a medical conference. He and his wife were as thrilled to see us as we were to see them. We were able to explain our situation and they understood. Sadly we parted but I was able to send greetings to all our old friends in Crato.

For a while we worked with three other missionaries in Teofilo Otoni, while waiting on the Lord as to where to go next. Gordon made a journey to Sao Paulo, as he had heard that the Lord was greatly blessing that area. He met up with an American missionary who had been using a tent for evangelistic meetings, which was not yet a common practice in Brazil. Gordon wanted to see how it was accepted and was much impressed by the response of the people. The difficulty had been to get the people into our meetings, as Protestant churches were out of bounds to all Catholics. However, a tent, being neutral ground as it were, drew people in. The Good News, preached in the power and demonstration of the Holy Spirit, did the rest.

Our American friend was due to go home on furlough and he gave the tent to us. It was full of holes I might add! Gordon fetched Malcolm and I down from Teofilo Otoni and we stayed with the American missionary while looking for a house to rent. After prayer, it was decided to transport the tent to São Vicente, a coastal town a little to the south of São Paulo.

Around this time a Brazilian evangelist was being used of the Lord to preach the Gospel and heal the sick. He had a radio programme which really aroused interest. When the people of São Vicente found that the Englishman in the old tent was also preaching the Word of God and praying for the sick, with wonderful results, they flooded to the tent. Being the rainy season, conditions under the canvas were not too comfortable but this did not deter them.

Gordon fixed up a wooden platform and installed an ancient P.A. system. Unfortunately it was placed just beneath one of the bigger holes. For the first night or two, Gordon was surprised when people told him that when he laid his hands on them (one hand holding the microphone) they felt a shock going through their body. Many were healed of various illnesses and all experienced the shock when prayed for. Gordon couldn't understand it, until one night, when the rain was falling steadily, he stepped off the wooden platform with the microphone in his hand. Quickly he jumped back on. He had discovered the source of the shock; a short circuit which was soon remedied! People continued to be healed, although some of them couldn't understand why they didn't feel the shock as they were prayed for, like those healed in the earlier meetings! They seemed a little disappointed until Gordon explained.

We moved to a little house between Sao Paulo and Sao Vicente. It was in the country and very isolated. The Brazilian lady who rented it to us was kind enough to let us have some kitchen furniture, as we only had enough money to buy a second-hand bedroom suite. There was a large pool in the garden, which had once been stocked with fish, although the last tenant had sold most of them. As the pool was deep, eight feet in most places, I was frightened that Malcolm would fall in, and I couldn't let him out of the house unless I was with him. There was no electricity and I had to fetch water up in buckets from the pool. As Gordon was away for much of the time, I was alone a great deal. Malcolm and I only joined him for short periods, staying with a local Christian. We had no transport of our own.

How thrilling they were, those visits to Sao Vicente! I met one blind man who had been healed and saw another receive his sight. He was the brother of a priest. As he received his sight, he ran round the tent, pointing at people and naming the colours of their clothes. One night a three year old girl was brought to us by her mother. Her eyeballs were white - sightless. The mother affirmed her faith in the Lord for the complete healing of her child's eyes and Gordon prayed for her. The mother then led the child away.

The tent was full of happy people who had come to the Lord. Many had been healed of various diseases and were now regular members of the congregation. Baptisms in the sea took place from time to time. The Christian workers had their hands full, with all that the work entailed. Gordon was later joined by an American brother, Robert Funderburg, and his daughter Carol, who was in her mid-teens. Although newcomers to Brazil and not yet able to speak Brazilian, they were valuable assistants, both being good musicians. Bob played the trumpet and Carol the piano accordion. A little while later, the Lord brought us two dedicated Brazilians, Hermelindo Domingues and his wife Lourdes, who took over the work when the church had been set in order.

One night, several weeks after my first visit, a lady with a little girl came to the front. They seemed vaguely familiar but I couldn't remember when I had seen them before. The little girl looked up at us with beautiful, shining brown eyes. Then the mother spoke and asked us if we remembered praying for a little blind girl some time ago. She told us that after being prayed for that night, she had taken the child home. The next day a little black spot had appeared in each white eyeball and from then on the eyes developed a little more each day, until the little girl had two beautiful brown eyes and could see perfectly. How we all rejoiced!

FORTY-NINE

"SEEK FIRST THE KINGDOM OF GOD..." MATTHEW 6:33

Bob Funderburg lived with his wife, Frances, and their three teenagers in a town in the interior of São Paulo called Bragança Paulista. It was a difficult place to work and none who had gone there to minister had any success. After witnessing Gordon's ministry, Bob asked Gordon if he would consider moving to Bragança. By this time I was crying out to the Lord for a change of house. I yearned to take a more active part in the work, at Gordon's side, instead of remaining home. I also wanted a house with water laid on, if not electricity, and the removal of the danger posed to my son by the fish pool. In my prayer, I reminded the Lord that He had said that if we sought His Kingdom He would give us the things we needed - Matthew 6:33.

An incident took place later that made me pray even more fervently. One day my husband was crossing the pool on a narrow ridge that divided it. Unbeknown to him, Malcolm was following behind. Something made Gordon turn around and he saw Malcolm in the water, bottom up! He hastily pulled him out and, thank God, he was none the worse for his experience.

Gordon came home to stay for a few days after handing over the church in São Vicente to Hermelindo and Lourdes. He was tired and needed to rest and seek the Lord with me for our next step. Together we considered moving to Bragança, and went over by bus to spend a couple of days with the Funderburgs.

While there we met an American lady missionary who had been helping them. However, she now felt that she should return to the States. We had lunch with her at her home which was simple but appeared luxurious to me! The little house was set in a good-sized garden, on the edge of the town. Just before we left she turned to us and said, "How would you like to take over this house when I'm gone? The landlord will transfer the contract to you and I will leave everything in it for you if you can help me with my fare. I feel you should come here to work and that God will use you to break through with the Gospel."

I turned to Gordon and said, "This is the answer to our prayers. I asked the Lord to provide us with a home and furniture and this is it!" Gordon said that we would go home and let her have our answer in a couple of days. How thrilled I was! Why, the house had electricity and running water, a kerosene refrigerator, butane gas cooker and wonder of wonders, an old-fashioned washing machine! The place was simply but adequately furnished and only needed our bedroom suite to make it complete. Our sister was leaving bed-linen, cutlery and so on and we wouldn't need to buy a thing - just move in. How I praised the Lord! He clinched the deal for us by sending in the amount to supply the rest of our sister's fare - well below the value of the things she left us. We moved in without delay.

It was nice living near people again. Our house was surrounded by a wall enclosing sufficient land in which to plant a vegetable garden with enough left over for Malcolm and his friends to play in. Next door was a small dry-cleaning business owned by a Japanese couple. They had a little girl and two boys around Malcolm's age, who soon made friends with him and they spent many happy days together. The Japanese had no garden and so they were pleased for their children to play in ours.

The Funderburgs were keen for us to join their Mission. We'd always had problems up North, finding men to care for the churches we had established. Belonging to an organization, we realized, would almost eliminate these difficulties. Bob arranged for Gordon to visit the headquarters of the Pentecostal Church of God in the U.S.A. to meet the leading brethren. Malcolm and I remained in Brazil.

FIFTY

"THEY WILL LAY THEIR HANDS ON THE SICK..." MARK 16:17

Six months later, when Gordon returned we were still trying to rent a place in which to start meetings. We had agreed to join the P.C.G. From now on the Funderburgs and ourselves would be able to develop a strong, sound fellowship of churches, adequately cared for, - but still we had no place in Bragança! The Funderburgs had to move into Sao Paulo, as Ricky their son needed to go to the American school there. Gordon and I began to wonder if we were in the right place. However, as we sought the Lord one morning, He assured us, through the gift of tongues and interpretation, that He had many people in Braganca. Our hearts reassured, we waited with expectancy for Him to work on our behalf.

Soon after, a Presbyterian lady visited us. She said that she had a large room that she could let us have, free, if we would clean it up. We were overjoyed and Gordon got his whitewash ready and started on the job. Before he was halfway through, however, the conviction grew in him that he was wasting his time and energy! The Holy Spirit seemed to be saying to him that this was not to be the place. He finished the work as quickly as he could and hurried home. "Jackie, that is not the place for us," he said. Rather exasperated, I replied, "Then where is the place?"

The next day, as we were walking down the main street, we noticed that the builders had just put the finishing touches to a fine new building. It looked like a large warehouse and we wondered what it was going to be used for. "What a grand place to hold meetings!" Gordon exclaimed. "The rent will be high, though, even if the owner would let us have it, which is unlikely," I remarked. As we walked back past the place, Gordon said, "You know, Jackie, I feel I should go and see the landlord." I smiled but said nothing. I didn't want to discourage him. We went home after Gordon had obtained the address of the proprietor. That evening we committed the matter to the Lord, asking Him to open the door of that place for us or else to show us speedily where we were to go.

The next day we went to see the landlord, who had an apartment above the new building. Gordon broached the subject of the possibility of renting the place and the owner, a Spaniard, started to ask him questions as to why he wanted it and what we were going to do there. Gordon threw caution to the winds and spoke boldly about the Gospel and the power of God. The man listened attentively until Gordon had finished relating how Jesus still heals the sick. A gleam came into his eyes and he asked us to accompany him into one of the bedrooms, where a finely built young man lay motionless. "This is my son-in-law," explained the host. "He had a stroke which left him paralyzed all down one side. Please tell him what you have been telling me."

Gordon, moved with compassion, told the sick man about the love and grace of God, as manifested in the redemptive work of Jesus on the cross. He spoke of His free pardon for sinners and power to heal the whole man. Finally, he asked the man to give us a sign if he would like us to pray for him. The man, who could not speak, lifted his right hand in assent, and Gordon laid his hands on him in the Name of Jesus. Seemingly nothing happened, and the Spaniard told us to come back the next day to receive his answer concerning the building. We left and returned home, where we lifted the sick man to the Lord in prayer, reminding Him of His promise to heal those upon whom we laid hands.

The next morning, we went to the downstairs entrance to the Spaniard's apartment and rang the bell. Someone came bounding down the stairs and the door opened to reveal - the son-in-law! The man embraced Gordon and took us upstairs. There the Spaniard awaited us, smiling, and the son-in-law poured out his gratitude to God and to Gordon. His father-in-law then told us that we could have the hall for three months, for just a nominal rent. He explained that the Bank had been promised the tenancy after that time. We took our leave and walked home on air!

Our finances only allowed for the building of a simple wooden platform and a few backless benches. We put a sign across the front of the hall, announcing that meetings would be held there and that prayer would be made for the sick. The town hummed with the news.

FIFTY-ONE

"CAST OUT DEMONS..." MARK 16:17

The great day arrived. It seemed as though all the people in the area had come to town! The market was a hive of activity in the morning, and as we did our shopping, curious glances were thrown at us and people turned to make comments to their companions. Laughter often followed these remarks and we knew that the townspeople regarded us as a huge joke. Some, of course, were indignant that we should be allowed to preach in their town.

By the afternoon the main business had been done and people gathered in the cafés and squares to exchange gossip. As we walked down the main street, we passed groups that were obviously watching the building, waiting for us to arrive and open the doors. I must admit that I felt very small as I walked by Gordon's side, carrying my little piano-accordion, and I guessed he felt the same.

The groups parted to let us through to the entrance. As Gordon opened the doors, a little lady came to him, weeping. She was accompanied by two big farm-labourers who were carrying a tall, well-built young man. The lady stopped us and begged Gordon to do something for her son. She told us that he had been paralyzed from the waist down for eight years and also subject to fits. He was her only son.

Gordon explained that he had no special power and that only Jesus could help. At that point, the man was seized by a fit, and started convulsing there on the pavement, foaming at the mouth. Gordon placed his Bible on his head, and in the Name of Jesus, commanded the evil spirit to leave him, ordering the man to stand up and be whole. A hush came over the bystanders as all eyes were fixed on the dramatic scene taking place before their very eyes. The convulsions ceased and the young man's body became still, then he straightened up, loosed himself from the restraining arms of his bearers and stood upright. He started to jump up and down with joy.

His mother, this time crying tears of happiness, took his arm and accompanied by the two labourers came into the hall and sat on the benches. A few folk followed us in and we held our simple meeting. God moved in our midst and the young man and his mother accepted Jesus as their Saviour. After being hugged and cried over at the end of the meeting, we returned home for our evening meal.

That evening we had difficulty in getting into the hall. Crowds, standing, jammed the place. Nobody could sit down except those who were around the edge of the platform. Even more crowds extended to the other side of the street outside. There was an air of expectancy as we started singing simple choruses. Led by Gordon's vibrant voice, they began joining in. Those outside also joined in. Then Gordon preached.

It was like water falling on dry, ploughed-up soil. The life-giving words of Jesus sank into those simple hearts who for so many years had lived in ignorance and fear of the God who so wanted to bless them. As Gordon told of a Saviour who not only pardoned the repentant sinner but freed him from the power of Satan and sin, tears flowed from many eyes. When telling of the Jesus who healed all who came to Him, believing, and who was the same yesterday, today and forever, people started to push their way to the front for prayer.

First, Gordon called for those who wanted salvation to put up their hands. We looked over the sea of waving arms and Gordon prayed, short simple phrases, to be repeated after him. The hall was filled with voices thanking God for His free pardon and calling upon Him to come into their hearts and take over their lives. We never knew how many came to the Lord that night. Hands were going up outside the building too, as we could see through the open door.

Many were healed and shouts of joy and praise went up to God as people felt His power operate within their bodies. Hernias, cases of T.B., and cancer were healed. In the confusion we couldn't register the miracles that occurred. Finally, we closed the meeting and escaped home, after announcing that a meeting would be held the next night.

For three months the meetings continued every night of the week but one. Not a night passed but that some souls came to the Saviour. People were delivered from demon powers - spirits of suicide were cast out, and others which caused a type of epilepsy and madness. The sick received healing. Night after night people came on to the platform to tell what the Lord had done for them.

We sent an S.O.S. to Bob Funderburg and he came over from time to time to help. After a while the Lord raised up a fine Brazilian, Braga, who joined us in the work. He was the local Station Master and a wonderful trumpet player. Before his conversion he was an alcoholic, and he would play the trumpet at the carnivals for more than two days nonstop. However, he finally had delirium tremens so badly that the doctor said he would soon die or go into a mental hospital. Then a Christian visited him and told him about Jesus. Braga, in desperation, turned to Him and was fully delivered from his drinking habit immediately. He was a wonderful witness to what God can do in a man's life.

FIFTY-TWO

The days passed in a whirl of activity. Country people were bringing their sick to our home, often arriving on our doorstep at seven in the morning. We were called to the bedside of infirm people all over town and we walked up hill and down dale to visit those needy ones. Even Gordon got thin! We cried out to the Lord for a vehicle and He moved the hearts of faithful friends back home to send us money for a jeep. Gordon started to learn to drive, receiving lessons from one of our converts - a tall good-looking young black man.

Just at this time, the Chief of Police sent for us to visit him. He was ill in bed with stomach ulcers and due to have an operation. When we got to his home, he asked us to pray for him. Gordon read the Scriptures to him and we prayed. The Chief felt the power of God working in his body and we rejoiced together. Within a couple of days we received news from the Chief, telling us that he was completely healed and eating well. Praise the Lord!

During the next few weeks Gordon must have broken half the rules in the book as he drove round but all we encountered were friendly policemen with advice or cautions! We learned later that our grateful Chief of Police had issued orders not to give us any tickets! In due time Gordon became a model driver, causing our friendly police no further embarrassment!

As people who lived outside town came in and became believers, so we received requests to go and hold meetings in other places. One man who surrendered his life to Jesus, begged us to go to his village, and opened his home for us to hold meetings. Only two or three people attended at first and we wondered about this.

Then, when we heard our new brother's testimony, we understood.

João had committed a violent murder and had been caught and sentenced to prison. As there was no capital punishment in Brazil, he was given a life sentence of which he served three years. However, being quite well-off, he was able to hire a clever lawyer who got him out of prison. He had later come to our meetings and met with Jesus.

Of course, knowing that he had been a man with a violent temper and possibly quite capable of killing again if provoked, his neighbours, not understanding the change in João, avoided him. After a few weeks, however, they realized the Lord had made a new man of him and started coming to the meetings. We soon had a thriving congregation in the place, with João as a loved and respected elder.

FIFTY-THREE

*"YOU SHALL BE MY WITNESSES IN JERUSALEM AND
ALL JUDEA AND SAMARIA..." ACTS 1:8*

Realizing that the radio was one of the best ways of reaching the people, Gordon tried to buy time on the local station. However, he was informed that our opponents had bought the station. Gordon then tried the radio station in Atibaia, a town twenty-five miles away. At first they were reluctant. Then I had the idea of offering to teach English free on their programme, if they would let Gordon preach. It worked, and we used tapes for the English lessons. The Gospel reached many people who had not dared to come to our meetings. After a time, some of these found courage to attend, and so the church grew. Our opponents did all they could to stop the people coming, writing scurrilous articles in the paper and speaking publicly against us. People were told to knock us over the head with their broomsticks if we came to their doors!

At Christmas, we placed a large tree in the hall, filled with little presents for the children. Most of these children had no other presents. Those women who could, made cakes and we had a great time of fellowship. During the evening, we saw a man put his head round the door. It was the local priest. His eyes grew round as he saw the tree and the people gathered round it, and he withdrew hastily! The next thing we knew, an article came out in the local paper accusing us of being descendants of the Druids, as we worshipped a tree!

Our three months had come to an end. Not being able to find a hall large enough to hold our growing congregation, we decided we would have to move into a big tent, which the Lord graciously provided, through the help of our supporters. The meetings were continued almost nightly for three years, after which time we were able to build a fine meeting-place. Braga proved to be a capable pastor. The congregations outside the town were growing too and Gordon was kept busy, taking the tent to places further afield. The Lord was moving in Brazil in a wonderful way.

FIFTY-FOUR

"I WAS IN PRISON AND YOU CAME TO ME." MATTHEW 25:36

One morning, not long after we had started the meetings in the main street, I went shopping. As I walked down the road, I saw a middle-aged black woman, tears running down her face. I stopped and spoke to her, asking why she was crying. She told me that she was a widow with one son, and had worked hard washing clothes to provide for them both. Having little time to watch over her teenage son, he had got into bad company without her knowing. A few days previously a policeman had come to her home and told her that the young man, now eighteen years old, had been caught stealing with his companions. He had been put in prison to await trial. As it was visiting day she was on her way to see him.

The gentle voice of the Holy Spirit within told me to accompany her, which I did, rather reluctantly, as I had a busy day ahead of me. As we entered the large iron gates and passed through the heavy door of the prison, the oppressive atmosphere enveloped us, added to the vile smells that assailed our nostrils. We joined the small group of people, mostly women, who stood by the iron grill of a large cell, trying to make contact with the men on the other side.

In the cell, in which there was only one window, high in the wall and covered by iron bars, there were about twenty men, ranging in age from sixteen to sixty. The cell was roughly twenty-five feet by forty and housed those guilty of offences ranging from vandalism to murder. No uniforms were provided, no soap to wash with nor toothpaste. In fact, all that was provided were some smelly mattresses and a few threadbare covers, which were brought out at night. In the morning, a husk of bread with a mug of black coffee was served for breakfast, while a meal of rice and beans was provided in the evening. There were never enough mattresses and covers to go around and some had to lie on the cold cement floor at night. As a result of the neglect, one man died not long after completing a couple of years there.

The men pressed to get near the grill, to speak to their visitors. One of the wives had two little ones holding onto her skirt. She looked thin and tired. It was hard on her and the other wives who had to earn a living somehow, while their menfolk were in jail. I stood to one side, during the visiting hour, but asked the guard if I could have a minute to speak to the prisoners, as the visitors were leaving. The guard I spoke to was my neighbour and his son played with mine. He gave me permission. I took note of the main needs of the prisoners as I spoke with them and told them who I was. Assuring them of my desire to help, I then left.

I turned out the few spare covers we had at home and then went round to various people I knew, asking for clothes and covers. By the next visiting day I had amassed quite a collection of things. Going early I saw the Chief Warden and asked him to provide more mattresses. He was rather embarrassed, I noticed, by the interest I was taking in the prisoners and I hoped that this would shame him into giving them the mattresses.

The men were very pleased with the things I had brought them and on the next visit a number of them greeted me warmly. I soon discovered that there were some who never received visitors. As they grew accustomed to my bi-weekly visits, those without visitors would insist on getting near to the grill for a couple of minutes for a chat with me. I took Malcolm and our dog in too, sometimes. The prisoners liked to talk to Malcolm. He spoke good Brazilian and in fact, I had trouble in getting him to study English!

Two or three made articles which their relatives would take and sell, thus getting a little money to buy food or other necessities. Because of the fighting that went on, however, few tools could be allowed in the cell because they would become lethal in the hands of the men. I talked over the situation with two of the prisoners. Idleness and boredom were among the causes of the fights. Not all could read and write, even if they did have literature brought in.

FIFTY-FIVE

"IS ANYTHING TOO HARD FOR THE LORD?" GENESIS 8:14

By this time, Gordon was getting the work organized and helpers were joining us. We had taken a young unmarried woman, who was expecting a baby, into our home. We paid for her to have her confinement in a small nursing-home, as girls in her situation were not treated very kindly in the local hospital. Her married aunt, who had no child, adopted the baby. She and her husband were Christians. Sebastiana, or 'Tiana' as we called her, responded to the love shown her and accepted Jesus as her Saviour not long after. She repaid our giving her a home by taking over the housekeeping almost entirely, thus releasing me to help more with the spiritual work. We paid her a proper wage of course, but she became a well-loved member of our family.

I took magazines into the prison, interspersed with tracts and Gospel literature. One tall, fine-looking black man, who was quite a leader among the prisoners, accepted the magazines but scorned the rest. I could see he was sceptical of what I was trying to do.

After a few weeks, I asked some of the men whether they would like us to hold a meeting in the prison. One said that several would but that they thought there was no chance of getting permission - the Prison Chaplain, though he never came near them himself, would never allow it. Officially, the Mayor of the town could grant me permission, but he would never do so for fear of the Chaplain. I told them that the Lord would make a way but I could see they didn't believe it!

Gordon and I prayed over the matter and I decided to visit the Mayor. He sent me to another official, to do with the Courts. Courteously he told me that he was not authorized to give me permission. He added that he thought that the prison was no place for a lady to visit. I replied that I went as an ambassador for Christ. The lawyer then said that if the Chaplain didn't think it worth him going there, what good could my visits do! Again I told him that if I took the message of Christ there, the Holy Spirit would do the rest. Still sceptical but looking a little uncomfortable, he showed me to the door.

Rather discouraged but determined not to give up, I sought the Lord and asked Him to make a way for me. I was moved by the plight of those poor men, incarcerated for months before their trial, with no exercise even in that wretched prison. They took it in turns to get on to each other's shoulders under the one window, so that they could see a little of the outside world and get a glimpse of the sun.

After a time of prayer with Gordon, I felt that I should visit the Mayor again. I found that he had wined and dined well and was drunk! As I explained my failure to get a permit, he waved his hand airily and said, "I can give you one, Senhora - no trouble, no trouble!" He proceeded to make out the necessary document and I left before he could sober up and change his mind!

I went straight to the Chief Warden of the prison and as I handed him my permit, his eyebrows lifted in surprise. I suddenly felt sorry for the Mayor - he was in for an uncomfortable time! The Warden smiled, rather nastily, and said smoothly, "My dear lady, I appreciate your desire to help the wretches down below but I'm afraid your efforts are wasted on the ungrateful creatures. I have just discovered a plot to escape. Some of the prisoners, led by the tall black fellow, had timed an escape to coincide with your next visit, so that they could use your body as a shield against our bullets! You will not want to bother with them any more will you?"

This announcement made by the Chief Warden came as a surprise, but did not deter me. I was more than ever persuaded of the need of these men, and told the Warden that we would be in the next day to hold a meeting.

FIFTY-SIX

"IF A MAN IS IN CHRIST, HE IS A NEW CREATURE"
II CORINTHIANS 5:17

The next day, we found some of the men subdued and sullen. However, as we sang one or two lively choruses, I saw that interest had been kindled. Gordon gave a simple Gospel message and this really made an impact on the men, who had never heard anything like it before. It was Gordon's first visit to the prison and he was greatly moved by the condition of the men and their surroundings.

At our next meeting, we took some young people into the prison with us to sing. We had to conduct our meeting in the hallway downstairs, and we were rather squashed, but the presence of the Lord was very real as we sang and ministered the Word. There was another cell down the passage, also, as well as a cell upstairs and a small one in which a woman prisoner would be put from time to time. Gordon made an appeal for men to accept Jesus as their Saviour. Two of them did so, to our great joy, and one of these was the black man who was the ringleader of the escape plot! We left a New Testament with each man and told them to pray together if they could manage it. I continued my visits in between the meetings and was now allowed in at almost any time.

Each week, more men came to the Lord. The Chaplain sent in a group of Daughters of Mary to catechize the prisoners, but they politely refused to take part. The opposition then tried other tactics, and the Warden told the men that they must sign a petition asking for our visits to be discontinued. He threatened them with punishment if they refused to sign. We had heard them whipping prisoners on several occasions, so knew what refusal to sign might entail. In spite of this, only three out of over forty signed. We all prayed and the threatened reprisals never took place, thank the Lord.

By this time, the atmosphere of the prison was changing. Far less fighting and swearing took place. The black brother, José would read the Scriptures aloud regularly, for the benefit of those who couldn't read. Then they would sing choruses. One of the guards, our neighbour, became a believer, as did two others, later.

During this time, I was also taking materials into the prison for the men to make into saleable goods. They made shopping bags, woven mats and toys. Wooden frames to make the mats were now permitted in the cell as the fighting was much less frequent. The Lord gave me favour with a carpenter who would give me a sackful of plywood periodically. This I would take to a young man who would cut it into shapes for me. He was an employee in a toy factory but did this work for me free. Carrying my sack of wooden shapes, paint and glue, I would make my way to the prison. There the prisoners would be eagerly waiting for me, glad to have some occupation to while away the long hours, and to have some money to give to their wives. My greatest problem was to sell the goods, however! At first I went round to the houses of the more well-to-do but I soon exhausted these contacts. Finally, I obtained a stall in the market. Unfortunately, the Brazilians, learning about the manufacturers of my goods would cut me down unmercifully in price until I barely covered the cost of the materials. It was a thankless task! I hated having to go back to the prison with such little money for the men who had put so much effort and care into the work they did, so we bought much of it ourselves.

We had been engaged for six months in the prison work and the fruits were obvious to all, including my sceptical lawyer! I was regarded as big sister by the youths and men, and was often called to the prison to help in some way or other. One day Gordon jokingly said, "Are you going to live up at the prison?" However, about thirty prisoners had their sentences cut down through good behaviour and several of those who had committed the worst crimes were sent to an agricultural camp. I received a letter from one of these, an ex-murderer but now a new creature in Jesus Christ. He said that he, and others, were meeting to read the Bible and sing choruses, and had asked permission to hold a baptismal service at a nearby river. He expressed his gratitude to us for having taken the Gospel to the prison. This letter became a treasured possession!

Finally, news came that the prison was to be closed as it was judged to be unsuitable as a place for long-term detention. Thankful as we were over this, when the time came to bid our prison brethren good-bye we were sad. Three of the young men were released and sent home. They joined our church, becoming responsible citizens. Some of the others were near the end of their sentences and assured us that they would seek out an evangelical church when they were released from the prison to which they were sent.

FIFTY-SEVEN

OUR SON PLAYS HIS PART

Sadness over parting with our spiritual sons was somewhat alleviated by the discovery that we were to have another baby. We had a little girl of two and a half, Miriam, in our home for a year. She had come to us in a dreadful state, her mother having abandoned her. The father had left the family earlier on. Miriam had now fully recovered and was a bonny little girl. We were told that we could adopt her and were just in the process of getting this done when her father appeared. He demanded that we give him the child, at the same time putting his hand on his gun! He had his eldest daughter, about seventeen years old, with him, who assured us that she would care for her little sister. So we sadly parted with Miriam, knowing that she would be returning to a life of poverty.

Now, however, we were to have another little one of our own. Malcolm was five and a half years old, and I had arranged a special correspondence course to enable me to teach him at home. At this time our landlord wanted to take over the house. We found another house on the outskirts of town which, although rather isolated, was on a lake and gave me a greater opportunity to rest and teach Malcolm. The demands on us had been heavy while living in the town.

Malcolm missed his friends, but his Dad managed to find time to teach him to fish. We also bought him a horse that was blind in one eye and a little lame, but Malcolm had some happy times with him! Then one day, the horse got into the neighbour's garden and wrought havoc among his vegetables. We had to sell the horse to pay for the damage!

While living in town, our young son had made his own contribution to the work. Sometimes he used to play with the son of the prison guard, a very nervous and fearful little boy. One day the guard said to me, "Since my son has been playing with your boy he has changed a lot. He is no longer fearful and nervous. Your Malcolm has helped him to get delivered from his fears by trusting in Jesus!"

A short time before the previous Christmas, Malcolm had told me that he wanted a fire-engine. I told him that it was impossible to get one of these in our area, so he should ask for something else. Malcolm said he would ask the Lord Jesus for one! I felt some trepidation over this, not wanting the boy to be disappointed and afraid that his simple faith might suffer. What little faith I had and how little I knew the goodness and understanding of our Lord! Christmas came and no fire-engine arrived but Malcolm although disappointed that it wasn't among his presents, affirmed that it would come - and it did, about ten days later! The Lord had put it upon the heart of a friend in England to send Malcolm a beautiful red fire-engine, complete with bell and ladders! How great is our God and how greatly to be praised! Malcolm was thrilled at being able to tell his friends how the Lord had answered his prayers! This made a big impression on the children of the neighbourhood and their parents.

When 'Tiana had been in the nursing-home, we went to visit her. While there, we met the owner, Dr. Ciuffo, and had a pleasant conversation with him, during the course of which I told him we had a five year old son. He said that he also had a son of five and that he would like to meet Malcolm. On his way home to lunch, he called at our house and asked Malcolm to have lunch with him and his family. I just had time to wash his hands and face and he was off! When the doctor brought him home he told us that before they ate, Malcolm had given thanks for his food, as was our custom, and had prayed for all the family! Dr. Ciuffo was much impressed and said that he would like our families to be friends. He and his beautiful wife were Italian, and so we were welcomed into this large, warm-hearted family. Later, the doctor, his wife and son, came into a personal relationship with the Lord Jesus.

FIFTY-EIGHT

A KNOTTY QUESTION

Of course, where should I go to have our baby but Dr. Ciuffo's nursing-home? He also had a book on the latest system of childbirth, which he lent me. The teachings of Dr. Lamaze are now an integral part of prenatal preparation, but how marvellous to find a practitioner of this method right in the interior of Brazil in 1960! How happy I was that I had been enabled to learn and practice this system because, when my time of delivery came, I was all alone! The doctor was demonstrating a Caesarean birth to Gordon in the operating theatre and the midwife was busy with the woman in the next room, but Linda was born without any problem, thank God. The midwife came in just as Linda entered the world! I never cease to be amazed at the leading of the Holy Spirit in every area of our lives!

Malcolm was brought in to see his little sister. He was really disappointed. "Mummy, I asked Jesus for a brother!" he exclaimed. "He sent a girl!" I sent up an SOS to the Lord and was given my answer. "Daddy had asked for a girl," I explained, "and because he is Daddy his prayer came first. When you are a daddy, your prayer will come first."

All the excitement of Linda's birth and Christmas which followed closely after was over. Our 'Tiana had married Jose, Gordon's driving instructor who was now a mature Christian. They were put in charge of one of our outposts. Everything in the mother church and other congregations was running well in the care of our national brothers. Gordon was becoming restive.

While visiting São Paulo one day, we were introduced to a Brazilian who had been the secretary of the Communist Party. Dr.

Luis Schiliró had come to the Lord as a result of an open-air meeting. He was an economist and a sort of 'trouble-shooter' for the banks. Luis had been told of the outpouring of the Holy Spirit in Bragança Paulista and urged Gordon to hold a meeting in São Paulo, for which he volunteered to make all the arrangements.

FIFTY NINE

Two weeks passed by and we were told that all was prepared for the meeting, which was to be held in a theatre in the centre of the city. When Gordon and I arrived, we found that the place was packed to capacity, with a jubilant Luis just 'raring to go'! After a few lively choruses, led by some local Christians, Gordon mounted the platform to give the message. The anointing of the Holy Spirit strong on him, he spoke of the power of Jesus to save, heal, and deliver from the power of Satan, and the crowd listened attentively.

Suddenly, just as he was closing the message, a very large woman started marching down the centre aisle towards him. She was calling out threats as she advanced, her anger being directed towards Gordon. "I have come to kill this man!" she shouted. Two stalwart missionary friends stepped out to intercept her, each taking an arm, but she lifted them off the ground and shook them off. Gordon, his first instinct being to look for the exit, suddenly remembered that Jesus had given us power over all the power of the enemy, and stood his ground, realizing that the woman was demon-possessed. He spoke to the demons in her, asking "How many are there of you?" "We are nine and we have come to destroy you'" they answered. Gordon began to command them to leave the woman, in the Name of Jesus. Luis had taken the microphone and, as a demon left, with a whistling sound, he announced it and the departure of every one that followed. Finally there was just one left, which defied Gordon, saying "This is my house and I'm not leaving." Gordon again took authority over it and, with a loud cry the demon left, while the woman sank to the ground unconscious. Luis burst into a chorus of praise to the Lord, while Gordon bent down and told the woman to rise, taking her by the hand. She opened her eyes and stood up, flinging her arms into the air and shouting "I'm free, I'm free - they've gone, praise God!"

Pandemonium then broke loose in the theatre! A man dashed to the front, crying out "It's gone, It's gone!" When Gordon asked him what had gone, he said that he had a large tumour in his side but that, as the last demon left the woman, he felt the tumour go down. Some other demon-possessed people were crying out and they were brought to the front, where Gordon ordered the demons to leave. Luis was behaving like the commentator at a football match, announcing the victory of Jesus over the demons as they left, one by one!

So many had come forward for prayer for healing that Gordon finally decided to make a general prayer for them all. Even as he prayed, one man shot his arm up - an arm that had been paralyzed, he told us afterwards. Others called out that hernias and other conditions were being healed.

Finally, we managed to close the meeting. Luis was crying with joy. He had never seen anything like this before. We then learned, that the theatre was next door to the voodoo centre!

"Brother Gordon, I will make arrangements for us to take the large sports stadium for some meetings," said Luis. Gordon did not feel that we were as yet ready to take on such a place. It would need much organization and many helpers. Reluctantly, Luis let us return to Bragance Paulista, where Gordon and I spent time waiting on God to know our next move.

CHAPTER SIXTY

"A LITTLE CHILD LEAD THEM" ISAIAH 11:6

As Gordon prayerfully considered the map of Brazil, the city of Belo Horizonte, in Minas Gerais, the heart of the country, became impressed upon him. He decided to take the tent to that large city. Together with another brother he conducted meetings there and the Lord greatly blessed the campaign. Then one night the tent was burned down! Happily the guard, sleeping in his hammock, escaped unhurt. Gordon came home fuming. We hadn't then learned to praise the Lord at all times and in all situations (Ephesians 5:20)! We took the matter to the Lord and the result was a gift from supporters to buy a bigger tent!

Gordon felt that we should move the family to Belo Horizonte, which we did. Linda was now three months old and Malcolm was six and a half. We found an American school in which we enrolled Malcolm and settled into our new home, sadly inferior to the one we had left behind but rents were high in this city. However, I was now ready again to take a more active part in the work.

The large tent was erected a central piece of waste ground much to the disgust of a number of University students, who had used the site for playing football. Gordon feared another attempt to destroy the tent, so we committed it to the Lord, asking for wisdom to deal with our adversaries.

As we started our meetings, I saw a number of young men hanging round the tent, and went outside to talk to them. Finding out they were students and keen on learning English, I offered to help them with their studies. From then on, we had no trouble, and several of them became believers and helped us, one looking after the sound system.

The first few meetings were not well attended. One night, however, a ten year old boy, who had been listening very attentively to Gordon's message, came up and asked us to pray for his mother, who had been bed-ridden for nearly eight years. We went to the boy's house the next morning and found the mother in bed, surrounded by pictures of saints on the walls. The little boy had told his mother all about the meeting and now asked us to tell his mother the Good News. The mother seemed eager to listen and just drank in all that Gordon said. We prayed for her afterward and then left. Two days later, the boy returned to the meeting beaming, accompanied by his mother walking with the aid of a stick. They came again the next night and this time she walked without the stick!

News of this healing got around and attendance grew. A poor woman came in one night, accompanied by her daughter. The mother had been found on several occasions, trying to commit suicide. Her son of eleven had killed himself a year before, after telling his family that he was being followed by a black demon. Since then the mother had the same urge. The daughter asked if we could help her. We certainly could, and in no time the woman was praising God for her deliverance.

The next night we stood just inside the tent entrance to welcome people, as usual. A large man came in and went straight up to Gordon with his hands held out to grasp his throat. Gordon just had time to call out "Jesus!" As he did so, the man stopped in his tracks and collapsed at Gordon's feet! He remained on the floor, unconscious for nearly three hours, until after the meeting, when he came to himself. Then Gordon went and cast the demon out of him in the Name of Jesus. The man did not remember what he had done, so Gordon spent a while with him, explaining what had happened. He told us that he was the son of the suicidal woman, and broke down weeping. Then he accepted Jesus as his Saviour.

We were able to buy time on the local radio and had a fifteen minute programme, three times a week, which reached roughly ten million people. Requests came in for visits to places round about.

With the tent congregation growing, house-meetings being held in the suburbs and now, calls for us to extend still further out, our days were full. The Lord raised up another worker, Timoteo, freeing Gordon to visit other areas.

SIXTY-ONE

One morning, Gordon came in to me and said, "Jackie, I have a burden for Portugal." Surprised I replied, "We have so much to do here that it will keep us busy for the rest of our lives. We can only pray for Portugal." With that, I'm afraid I dismissed the matter from my mind. There was so much demanding my attention. To my shame, I must admit that I did not think of Portugal again for another fifteen months.

Soon after this, Linda caught gastroenteritis. I had fed her myself for fifteen months hoping to strengthen her resistance to infection by so doing, but the dreaded disease struck her down. Conventional medicine produced no improvement in her condition and I prayed desperately. My memory of the ordeal I had gone through with Wendy, our firstborn was revived. Just then, we met a missionary who told us of a homeopathic doctor who had helped her a great deal. We took Linda to him and his treatment produced quick results. Linda recovered but remained frail.

It was time for us to go home on furlough and Linda's weakened state of health forbade delay. As we made preparations to leave, Gordon vowed that this would be our last furlough. We would return to Brazil, never more to leave the country! A missionary friend was going to watch over everything for us during our absence, and we reluctantly bade farewell to our dear church family.

SIXTY-TWO

A PROPHECY AND A VISION

After a couple of month's rest spent with friends we were ready to do some itinerating. Gordon went on his own, first of all, and one of the places he visited was South Chard Christian Church in Somerset, where he had a very blessed time. Then Malcolm caught chicken-pox! How could we itinerate with a sick child and an infectious one at that! We had to leave the rented house which my Aunt had taken for us for a few weeks. Gordon, in desperation, telephoned the Manor House at South Chard and asked for prayer for our situation. Auntie Mil's cheerful voice said, "Bring the family down here, chicken-pox and all!" - which we did. How thankful I was to be able to stay in that welcoming home! We all quickly settled in and became part of that loving, caring church, staying there for three months.

Uncle Sid and Auntie Mil Purse, as they were called, had sold up their prosperous guest-house and bought an ancient thatched-roofed Manor House complete with large barn and shed for their Jersey cow. Uncle Sid, being a builder, turned the barn into a beautiful church building. During Gordon's first visit, the Lord poured out His Spirit upon the small group that gathered there. The Manor House was open to all those who came needing help and the group began to grow.

Auntie Mil, who had no children of her own, took little Linda, now two and a half, under her wing. Every day she took Linda with her to milk the cow and Linda drank bottles and bottles of that rich liquid, growing stronger and plumper every day. We all appreciated Auntie Mil's care and good cooking and Malcolm thrived on it, joining the local village school as soon as he was well.

One day Auntie Mil was in the kitchen and she had a sudden vision of Linda standing on the ledge of an open upstairs window. She dashed upstairs and saw Linda standing on the window ledge she had seen in her vision. Quietly she lifted her down thanking God fervently for His intervention.

Another day, a visiting boy hurt his leg and Linda went and prayed for him as she had seen her Daddy do. Some other boys thought they would have some fun with Linda so they asked her to pray for them. Linda quickly saw what they were up to, so as they came up to her she hit them sharply and then prayed for them. The laugh was definitely on them!

Just before the end of the three months, a Scottish sister came to South Chard. She was a prophetess and one night she prophesied over me and told me of trials and sorrows yet to come. I was devastated - hadn't we had enough tribulation already?

The next morning, at a small prayer-meeting in the church, I recalled Barbara Massey's words and thought back on what we had gone through in our first term in Brazil. I couldn't go through anything like that again; resentment and rebellion rose up in my heart towards the Lord. Suddenly I had a vision of the head of Jesus, with His eyes looking straight at me. Those eyes were full of love and understanding and, as I met their gaze, all the rebellion seeped out of me. I could only weep before Him and yield myself to Him anew, for Him to do with me as He wished. The vision faded and afterward I couldn't tell anyone what His hair was like or anything else, but the remembrance of His eyes have remained with me always.

Linda in the meantime, had contracted German measles. Shortly after her recovery we left South Chard and Uncle Sid drove us to Southampton to sail for the U.S.A. Unhappily, I was unable to enjoy the delicious food on the ship as I was sick for most of the voyage!

We travelled by train from New York to Kansas and from there to Wichita, where we were warmly welcomed by our American brethren. They installed us in the Missionary Home and Malcolm was enrolled at the local school. After a few days Gordon, Linda and I started out on our itinerary, while Malcolm remained in the care of the dear sister who had donated the Missionary Home, and now lived next door. Just before leaving, I visited the doctor who confirmed my suspicions. What I had thought had been sea-sickness was in reality pregnancy sickness!

SIXTY-THREE

*"WHEN YOU PASS THROUGH THE WATERS,
I WILL BE WITH YOU..." ISAIAH 43:2*

After an enjoyable and profitable few months with Gordon, Linda and I returned to Wichita. In due time I was taken to the big Methodist Hospital for the delivery of the baby and all went well. I was concerned however, that little Priscilla didn't cry like the others. I could hardly hear her. After a short time, we realized that she was ill. In spite of prayer, her condition worsened and we took her back to the hospital. Thorough examination revealed that she had two holes in the heart. As we stood at the bottom of the bed the doctor said, "I'm afraid that you will never take this baby back to Brazil." Without recognizing the implication of his words, I said, "Then we will take her to Portugal!"

Due to the high cost of operating on 'Cilla in the USA, we were advised to take her back to England. Our faithful P.C.G. churches paid the hospital bills and we took her on the plane, with oxygen apparatus at hand. As we had already told our British Consul about our situation, when we arrived in England we were met by an ambulance which took us to the Great Ormond Street Hospital in London. Once there her condition worsened and they decided to operate. The surgeon was only able to bind the pulmonary artery, to relieve the shunting of blood in her heart. He said he would operate again when she was older. After six weeks we brought her home.

While still in America, wondering where we could go to live on our return to England, a letter had arrived. A friend of ours in Devonshire had recently been widowed. Knowing nothing of our circumstances but that we were presumably preparing for our return to Brazil, she wrote that, should we ever need a home in England, hers was open to us! We wrote and told her of Priscilla's condition, and asked if we could come to her on our return to England. She replied by return of post, assuring us of a warm welcome. Once again the Lord had sent His angels to prepare the way!

For some weeks we stayed in Flo Mayums home and then the Lord made it possible for us to buy the house next door! In the meantime, an American brother wrote to us saying that he and his wife were in Portugal. They were having problems and, as they were only beginning to learn the language, they needed someone who could speak fluently. The Mission Director asked Gordon to visit them, which he did. On his return to England, we discussed the situation. We remembered the time just over a year ago, when the Lord had put Portugal on Gordon's heart and how in the hospital, at the side of Priscilla's bed, I had spontaneously declared that we would go to Portugal! The Pentecostal Church of God Mission Board had very kindly told us that we could work in Europe, as our child's health permitted. It was decided that Gordon should go to Portugal and take the place of the Chinns, while they would go to Brazil. The children and I were to join Gordon when possible.

While in the USA we had been enabled to raise the money to build a Bible School and Orphanage in Brazil. The Chinns took this project on, while Gordon sadly looked to the Lord to guide him in his new sphere. Just as he was preparing to return to Portugal, Priscilla developed meningitis. I told Gordon to go ahead, while I spent my time between the hospital and home. 'Cilla recovered in due time but was now helpless.

The muscles in her chest and back were affected by what was called hypertonia. This little girl was unable to use her legs and had only limited movement in her arms, with insufficient strength to feed herself.

I sadly considered our situation and wondered how we could continue with our missionary calling with an invalid child. One day as I was washing the dishes, the Lord spoke to me and told me to take the family to Portugal. I wrote to Gordon and told him to prepare a home for us.

SIXTY-FOUR

"GIVE AND IT SHALL BE GIVEN TO YOU..." LUKE 6:38

It was decided that Malcolm, now ten and a half, should go to the Emmanuel Grammar School, in Swansea as a boarder. This school had been founded for the children of missionaries. I had not as yet experienced the pain of separation from my children and I felt this deeply but knew that it was the best arrangement for Malcolm. Linda was four years old and I decided I would teach her at home.

We had no car but were saving up for a second-hand one and had £25 towards it. An evangelist friend came to stay with us whose car needed repairs, and he had no money to pay for them. Gordon had just returned from Portugal and we were wondering how to move the family out there. However, learning of our brother's need, Gordon looked at me meaningfully and I nodded. We would give him our £25. We knew the Lord would provide for us in some way or other.

Less than a month later, we learned that a Plymouth Estate car was on its way over to us from America! The dear ladies of the churches over there had saved up Green Shield Stamps and taken them to the Chrysler car firm, who gave them a great reduction in price when they learned the destination of the car! The Lord wonderfully undertook for the import tax, which the Customs kindly wavered. Gordon lacked only two weeks to complete time spent out of the country, needed for tax exemption. Soon we were busy packing as many household items as we could into this beautiful, spacious car, with a mattress of top for Linda to lie on. The hospital had agreed to keep Priscilla two weeks longer while we set up home in Portugal, after which time I was to return for her and take her back by plane.

SIXTY-FIVE

"THE LORD IS THEIR STRENGTH, AND HE IS THE SAVING STRENGTH OF HIS ANOINTED." PSALM 28:8

During the two years since 'Cilla's birth, Gordon had felt unable to pray for the sick, so shattered was he by the fact that the Lord did not heal our precious daughter. Then one day, before we left for Portugal, Gordon was preaching at a church in Wales, where the Lord had already blessed his ministry. At the close of the meeting, a brother brought his little boy of five and sat him on Gordon's lap just as he had finished speaking. The child was paralyzed from the waist down as a result of having had polio. "Please pray for my son," the brother said. Gordon looked at him and then spoke to the Lord. "You know how I feel," he said, "this child is in Your Hands." The Lord replied, "It is I Who do the healing." The boy got up from Gordon's lap and ran to his father. Gordon wept. The same boy is now a naval officer on a large ship. From then on, Gordon knew he must continue in the ministry the Lord had given him.

As we settled in our sparsely furnished house in Portugal, we looked to the Lord to guide us, as we had always done. We knew that He would not fail us. Our work in Brazil was finished and a new task lay ahead of us. With our lively four year old and little invalid, we waited to see how He would work.

Portugal was then fifty years behind the rest of Europe and ruled by the iron hand of a dictator. Evangelization had to be conducted within strict limitations. No name could be put outside a church building and only a few could gather at a time in house-meetings. Believers were second-class citizens. Four out of five men were employed by the government, many as National Guards. Illiteracy was 90%. Wages were low but anyone heard complaining about the situation would be whisked off by the National Guards and never seen again. Informers were given a small reward. The very atmosphere was oppressive!

As we tried to adapt to the customs of the country, we also had to change our speech. We were told that we spoke Brazilian and therefore, 'black' Portuguese! The people were suspicious and so different from our courageous, hospitable Brazilians! Even the Christians we met were very legalistic and lacking in love toward one another. It was a depressing situation. As I looked at my helpless two-year old daughter I prayed for strength and grace.

During those early months, when the children were in bed at night, we would often look back over the years spent in Brazil and reflect on the way the Lord had kept and provided for us. As young Christians we had stepped out on what was, to us, an uncharted course. In our tribulations and our triumphs we were to be 'living letters from Christ ... read by everybody.' Living among the poor, subject to the same hardships and dangers, our way of life was open to the inspection of all. As we passed through one trial after another, we testified to those around us of the faithfulness of the Lord to His promises, made to all who would put their trust in Him. We were living proof that His angels did indeed "camp around us" (Psalm 34:7) and did cause things to happen to change our circumstances.

The verse that the Lord gave me when I asked Him for a title for this book, sums it up well. "For He will give His angels (especial) charge over you, to accompany and defend and preserve you in all your ways (of obedience and service)." Psalm 91:11 Amp.

Meditating on these Scriptures and our past experiences, Gordon and I strengthened each other and ourselves in the Lord. How could we doubt the desire and ability of our Lord to direct us in new paths of service in this needy land? The prophesy made over me in South Chard came to my mind, and I recalled the way Jesus had looked at me the morning after, when I was sitting before Him full of fear and resentment. Together Gordon and I resolved that we would continue to serve Him, however hard the way, because He had promised never to leave us nor forsake us. We continued to wait expectantly for Him to guide us in these new paths.